Praise fo

D0725579

"Vermeulen has put together an amazing compendium of interesting, counterintuitive, and sometimes disturbing findings about management. He delivers the material in succinct, readable, and often humorous prose, and illustrates his points with compelling examples. The result is a uniquely valuable book that will be informative and entertaining to a variety of corporate 'stakeholders', which in the end includes all of us."

James Westphal, Robert G. Rodkey Collegiate Professor of Business Administration; Professor of Strategy, University of Michigan, Ross School of Business

"This book is a delicious read. Freek Vermeulen presents us with a candy dish of witty reflections about the current state of management in a candid and disarming personal tone. His knack for cutting through to the essence of complex ideas and stripping them of a sometimes undeserved pomposity is truly impressive; it delivers an enlightening wealth of conversation starters for managers. Two thumbs up!"

Gabriel Szulanski, Professor of Strategy, INSEAD

"Freek is one of those rare people who manage to combine real substance with flair, making complex insights highly understandable. He is one of those people who make you feel smarter. He offers a fresh, honest and atypical way to look at management issues that few people take the time to stop and analyse. This book will not disappoint you. Vermeulen decodes and translates business research with intelligence and wit. He uses his extensive knowledge of both research and the practice of management to compile a fascinating overview of the latest insights from management science.

Business books often seem to have a questionable base to them, lacking solid evidence for their recommendations. Not this one. *Business Exposed* builds on facts and research. Freek's style is hardly that of a stuffy professor though: it is fast, sharp and with a great sense of humour."

Ruby McGregor-Smith, Chief Executive Officer, MITIE Group plc

"*Business Exposed* is a delight! Using fast-paced analysis and insights from academic research as well as humour and plain common sense, it exposes the naked truth behind many of the things that we take for granted in business. In the process, it disrobes the emperor of conventional wisdom to reveal how things really work in the strange business of business. Vermeulen is a master story teller and this book is a testament to that. It will change the way you think of business for good."

Costas Markides, Professor and holder of the Robert P. Bauman Chair in Strategic Leadership, London Business School

"If the role of CEO is chief storyteller, Vermeulen's role is chief doubter. He is the boy laughing at corporate kings with no clothes on. But he makes sure we all laugh with him. And that we'll never look at business in the same way again."

Stevie Spring, Chief Executive Officer, Future plc

"Wow, what a book! It's fresh, informative, and funny. It's chock full of insights that you won't expect. After reading it, you'll never think about your business in the same way again.

Every so often a book comes along that re-frames business. *Business Exposed* does just that in a fast-paced, smart read based on serious research. You'll find yourself re-thinking and changing what you do."

Kathleen M. Eisenhardt, Stanford Warren Ascherman Professor of Strategy and Organization, Stanford University

"This deeply insightful and in places controversial book will be of great interest to managers and observers of business. It does a wonderful job of distilling insights from research on human behavior and applying it to business to show how managers can sometimes systematically deviate from rational behavior."

Ranjay Gulati, Jaime and Josefina Chua Tiampo Professor of Business Administration, Harvard Business School

"Professor Freek Vermeulen is that rare academic who not only has a great command of his field but also can make management research highly accessible to everybody. His book exposes the many silly things that go on in business; you can improve your performance greatly if you understand and correct those. *Business Exposed* is not only an eye-opener but also highly entertaining!"

Morten T. Hansen, Professor of Management, University of California, Berkeley and Professor of Entrepreneurship, INSEAD

Business Exposed

The naked truth about what really
goes on in the world of business

Freek Vermeulen

Financial Times
Prentice Hall
is an imprint of

Harlow, England • London • New York • Boston • San Francisco • Toronto • Sydney • Singapore • Hong Kong
Tokyo • Seoul • Taipei • New Delhi • Cape Town • Madrid • Mexico City • Amsterdam • Munich • Paris • Milan

PEARSON EDUCATION LIMITED

Edinburgh Gate
Harlow CM20 2JE
Tel: +44 (0)1279 623623
Fax: +44 (0)1279 431059
Website: www.pearsoned.co.uk

First published in Great Britain in 2010
© Freek Vermeulen 2010

The right of Freek Vermeulen to be identified as author of this work has been
asserted by him in accordance with the Copyright, Designs and Patents Act 1988.

Pearson Education is not responsible for the content of third party internet sites.

ISBN: 978-0-273-73292-1

British Library Cataloguing-in-Publication Data
A catalogue record for this book is available from the British Library

Library of Congress Cataloging-in-Publication Data
Vermeulen, Freek.
  Business exposed : the naked truth about what really goes on in the
world of business / Freek Vermeulen.
    p. cm.
  ISBN 978-0-273-73292-1 (pbk.)
  1. Management. 2. Business planning. 3. Decision making. I.
Title.
  HD31.v44 2010
  658--dc22
                                                        2010032836

ARP Impression 98

Typeset in 9/13pt ITC Stone Sans by 3
Printed in Great Britain by Clays Ltd, St Ives plc

Contents

8   A rock or a soft place? / 194

About the author

Freek Vermeulen is an Associate Professor of Strategic & International Management at the London Business School, where he teaches on the MBA and Executive levels. He has designed and taught some of the School's most successful courses such as Strategic Management, General Management, Strategies for Growth, and Mergers, Acquisitions & Alliances which, in combination, earned him the School's "Best Teacher Award". In addition, in 2008, he was announced as the first ever recipient of London Business School's "Excellence in Teaching Award".

Over the past years, Freek has acted as an advisor and worked on executive programmes for companies such as BP, EDS, The Guardian, the Fiat Group, IBM, KPMG, Lloyd's, Maersk, Novartis, PwC, Roche, Sara Lee, ThyssenKrupp, Toshiba, Vodafone, and various others. He is also a much sought-after keynote speaker on company and industry conferences, covering topics such as strategic innovation, execution, stimulating growth, and international strategy. In 2009, the *Financial Times* wrote about Freek: "The London Business School associate professor is a rising star and his pithy observations are both accessible and authoritative".

Freek's research on strategies for growth has been published extensively in highly reputed academic journals, such as the *Academy of Management Journal, Administrative Science Quarterly*, and the *Strategic Management Journal*. As a result, he received the prestigious "Academy of Management Journal Best Paper Award" for his research on international expansion. In addition, his views on management appeared in global practitioner outlets, such as the *Harvard Business Review, Sloan Management Review*, and the *Wall Street Journal*. He also wrote a popular business blog for the *Harvard Business Review* (called "Strategy Freek"), which was covered in *Business Week*, *The Washington Post*, and the *Financial Times*, among others.

He currently serves on the editorial boards of the *Academy of Management Journal*, *Organization Science*, *Strategic Organization*, and the *European Management Review*. He is a member of the Strategic Management Society and the Academy of Management, and served on the Advisory Council of the Academy of Management Journal. Freek obtained a PhD in business administration ("cum laude") from Tilburg University and a PhD in Organization Studies from Utrecht University in the Netherlands.

Publisher's acknowledgements

Picture Credits

The publisher would like to thank the following for their kind permission to reproduce their cartoons:

Roger Beale: pages 79, 113, 130, 206; **Dave Carpenter:** pages 21, 55, 80, 142, 171, 177; **Dave Coverly:** pages 4, 31, 64; **Mike Shapiro:** pages 106, 210

Text

Quote on pages 74–5 from WAR AND PEACE by Leo Tolstoy, translated with an introduction by Rosemary Edmunds (First published in Penguin Classics in two volumes 1957, Reprinted with revisions 1978). Copyright © Rosemary Edmunds 1957, 1978.

Introduction: The monkey story

The experiment involved five monkeys, a cage, a banana, a ladder and, crucially, a water hose.

The five monkeys were locked in a cage, after which a banana was hung from the ceiling with, fortunately for the monkeys (or so it seemed …), a ladder placed right underneath it. Of course, immediately, one of the monkeys raced towards the ladder, intending to climb it and grab the banana. However, as soon as he started to climb, the sadist (euphemistically called "scientist") sprayed the monkey with ice-cold water. In addition, however, he also sprayed the other four monkeys …

When a second monkey was about to climb the ladder, the sadist would again spray the monkey with ice-cold water, and apply the same treatment to its four fellow inmates; likewise for the third climber and, if they were particularly persistent (or dumb), the fourth one. Then they would have learned their lesson: they were not going to climb the ladder again, banana or no banana.

In order to gain further pleasure or, I guess, prolong the experiment, the sadist (scientist) outside the cage would then replace one of the monkeys with a new one. As can be expected, the new guy would spot the banana, think, "Why don't these idiots go get it?!" and start climbing the ladder. Then, however, it got interesting: the other four monkeys, familiar with the cold-water treatment, would run towards the new guy – and beat him up. The new guy, blissfully unaware of the cold-water history, would get the message: no climbing up the ladder in this cage – banana or no banana.

When the beast outside the cage replaced a second monkey with a new one, the events would repeat themselves – monkey runs towards the ladder, other monkeys beat him up, new monkey does not attempt to climb again – with one notable detail: the first new monkey, who had never received the cold-water treatment himself (and didn't even know anything about it), would, with equal vigor and enthusiasm, join in the beating of the new guy on the block.

When the researcher replaced a third monkey, the same thing happened; likewise for the fourth until, eventually, all the monkeys had been replaced and none of the ones in the cage had any experience or knowledge of the cold-water treatment.

Then, a new monkey was introduced into the cage. It ran toward the ladder, only to get beaten up by the others. Yet, this monkey turned around and asked, "Why do you beat me up when I try to get the banana?" The other four monkeys stopped, looked at each other slightly puzzled and, finally, shrugged their shoulders: "Don't know. But that's the way we do things around here."

This book

My friend and colleague at the London Business School, the illustrious Costas Markides, used to tell the executives in his classroom this story. It reminded him – and me – of quite a few of the organizations we have seen over the years. That's because the world of business is full of habits (and I guess full of monkeys …): habits we take for granted and never question.

Yet, some of them are actually quite strange, and some of them simply don't work. Has it ever occurred to you that there is quite a gap between how companies make and pretend to make big strategic decisions? Doesn't it sometimes strike you as strange that our boards of directors are really a bunch of part-timers and amateurs? Do you really think the "Chinese walls" in investment banks are as impermeable as they say they are when they make stock recommendations to us for the same firms that are their clients? Don't you think it might be a tiny teeny little bit odd that often no less than 80 percent of a CEO's remuneration consists of stock options which we know from research greatly enhance risk-taking behavior, while at the same time we seem to yearn for CEOs who are a bit more risk-conscious? And, while we're at it, why do so many of them seem to be plain narcissistic egomaniacs?

I don't know about you, but I have also wondered why new bandwagons of management fads (such as "Six Sigma" or "Empowerment" or "Managing by Objectives") continue to roll across the corporate landscape. Why do herds of consultants seem to eagerly use downsizing for all corporate ailments in the same way that medieval quacks employed bleeding as a cure for all possible diseases? And why do we persistently see surges of acquisitions in most industries while research conclusively shows they lose money? I could go on and on and, frankly, I will. But my point is that there really are quite a few things in the world of business that we take for granted, that we seldom consider or talk about, but that I think are worth stripping down and exposing for what they are, so that we can ask ourselves whether they really are a sane "way of doing things round here".

Hence, in this book, I will reveal what really goes on inside business, explore what CEOs really are like, and dissect the temptations, the influences, and the (sometimes ill-advised) liaisons and strategies of corporate life.

Yet, don't be mistaken; although I think I have succeeded in keeping it relatively light and, above all, fast-paced, this entire book is nevertheless explicitly based on rigorous research and verifiable facts. Because that's what I am; a scientist who examines managers just like a criminologist studies criminals, and a zoologist might study mountain gorillas (or monkeys in cages). I analyze their behavior and reveal what really goes on in their world; who makes it, who doesn't, and why things work the way they do.

This also means that this is not a business book. You may have found it in the business book section of Waterstones or WH Smith but, I am sorry, it really is not a business book. It is a book *about* business. And this is not just some semantic gimmickry. Business books tell you what to do (if you want to make it big in business). They are the "how-to" books for people who wear pin-striped suits and ties, which tell you that the author (invariably labeled "management guru") thinks – pardon, knows – you should do X, after which he or she proceeds with another 124 pages of examples of companies or people that made it big precisely by doing X. I am not going to tell you X. I am not going to tell you what to do. I am going to tell you how things work, in the strange business of business.

Yet, I do think that, if you want to make it big (and there is no reason to be ashamed of that!), you'd better understand how things work, in the kingdom that you are trying to rule. Because don't be mistaken, the things that I will reveal to you concern the fundamental nature of business today. They cut through conventional perceptions of how business works to show you what really goes on, and how that affects firm performance. They explain how success today can mean failure tomorrow; who becomes a corporate hero and who becomes a villain; and how money gets made – and lost. As such, I hope my analysis will build your understanding of today's corporate world from the ground up.

So, if you're in business yourself, polish up your business savvy with my little exposé. If you're a curious observer, I hope you will be entertained (and sometimes slightly appalled …) by the hidden facts and realities revealed.

Freek Vermeulen

Management happens

Forced to be stupid

essica Nolan, a researcher at the University of Arkansas, was interested in persuading residents of a particular California community to conserve more energy at home. For this purpose, she designed four types of notes, to be delivered to people's homes. These notes (roughly) said the following:

1 Do it because it helps the environment
2 Do it because it benefits society
3 Do it because it saves you money
4 Do it because everybody else is already doing it.

Before using the notes, she knocked on a number of residents' doors and asked them which of the four arguments would most likely persuade them. Pretty much everybody said, "Not the fourth! (I care about the environment, I care about society, I certainly care about money, but I couldn't care less about what everybody else is doing)". But did they?

Subsequently, Jessica sneaked out at night and hammered one of the four notes on each door in the community.

Some time after that, she went back to check people's meter readings. And guess what: households that had received the fourth note ("Everybody else is doing it") had by far the biggest reduction in energy consumption.

We are hugely affected in our decision-making and behavior by our notion of what others are doing, although we usually don't quite realize it (and deny it vigorously!). We might think that we don't care what others are doing but the reality is: we do. It is only human.

Even top managers can be almost human (or at least some of them). For example, there is a lot of research on what influences managers' strategic decisions (e.g., whether to choose strategic option A or B). And guess what, it's imitation.

❝ Even top managers can be almost human (or at least some of them). ❞

There is research on where firms choose to locate their new plants, whether or not they enter a particular market, adopt a new type of organizational structure, a governance instrument, etc, etc. Consistently, results show that managers are led by one simple question: "What are my competitors doing?" And then they just do the same thing.

The problem is, sometimes what your competitors are doing is stupid. For example, research has indicated that (in certain industries) ISO 9000 quality norms are counter-productive. Yet, throughout the 1990s firms imitated each other anyway and adopted the system.

And it gets worse. Sometimes, if you're the only one that does not adopt the new practice, you start to look "illegitimate". Analysts, shareholders, customers, and so on start asking questions: "Everybody else is doing it; shouldn't you?" "Surely, everybody else cannot be wrong". But they can!

In this case – because customers start to shun them, investors criticize them, analysts downgrade them, etc. – firms may actually start to suffer from not having adopted the silly practice. This places pressure on the firm to also act stupid, just to fit in, and be accepted. It takes a brave firm to stop such a vicious cycle of imitation.

Collective inertia – if you don't join them, you can beat them!

The inclination to conform to the behavior of others can sometimes lead to some mighty strange and plain irrational situations in the world of business. For example, have you ever wondered why newspapers are so ridiculously big? Perhaps when you were trying to read one in your garden on a sunny yet windy afternoon, forcing you to peel the pages off your face every three seconds? Or while reading one on the train, smashing your elbow in a nodding neighbour's face when turning the page? I did. Not smashing my elbow in anyone's face, but wondering why these pages had to be so bloody large. I simply assumed that it was much cheaper to print on large pages than small ones. Turns out I was wrong.

To my surprise, I found out that printing on large pages is actually more expensive than on smaller ones! Why did they do it then; are these *Times*, *Guardian* and *Daily Telegraph* people closet sadists, finding secret joy in making us struggle daily with inky pages? Here's what happened. In 1712 British newspapers came to be taxed on the number of pages published. Editors then decided to print the news on enormous pages, and fewer of them, creating the broadsheet format. The original tax disappeared in 1855 but, despite being considerably more expensive, the format persisted.

As you may remember (if you're from London), a couple of years ago, after the free newspaper *Metro* entered the industry, *The Independent* was the first to abandon the broadsheet and "go tabloid". Their sales figures surged. Soon *The Times* followed, and later also *The Guardian*, all to their benefit. But why did it take so long? Had no-one ever conceived the idea of printing newspapers on smaller (and cheaper!) pages?

Sure they had. Many times over the years someone would bring it up: "Shouldn't we print on smaller pages?" But they would always dismiss the idea: "No-one is doing it" and, mostly, "The customer would not want it" but we did!

I call this "collective inertia". Every existing player in the industry was afraid to break the mold and take the plunge. I have also learned, studying many firms in many different lines of business, that most industries have similar idiosyncracies that everybody adheres to but nobody really remembers why we're doing it that way.

But hardly anyone dares to challenge it. And that is where the business opportunity lies. If you're the first one to spot the silly convention (just to name a few candidates: buy-back guarantees in book publishing, detailing in the pharmaceutical industry, insane working hours in investment banking) and do it differently, it might just make you a heck of a lot of money.

And it would save many of us customers from a daily elbow in the face.

Pharma – the devil is in the detailing

Let me give you an example of what I think might be a case of "collective inertia", although admittedly I have no hard evidence of such. But they sometimes do seem like a bunch of monkeys (staring at a banana): pharmaceutical companies.

What do you think pharmaceutical companies spend most of their money on? R&D: the search for new drugs? Think again.

True, pharma companies spend a great deal on R&D; studies show it makes up about 14 percent of their revenue. Yet, they spend about a third of their revenues on marketing. That's right, on average, pharmaceutical companies spend two to three times as much on the marketing of a drug as on its development. (Hence, next time you hear a pharma executive claim they need to charge such a high price for drugs because of the high costs of R&D, frown at him fiercely!)

By far the largest chunk of these marketing expenses are taken up by the practice of "detailing"; that is, a vast army of company representatives visits physicians to shower them with information, free samples, and persuasive arguments (and a "healthy dose" of free gifts and travel), claiming that the company's drug is wonderful and really does what it says on the tin. The raison d'être of this practice is that physicians – human as they (often) are – only remember and hence only prescribe a limited number of drugs; much fewer than are in existence. Therefore it is important for a pharma company to make sure that physicians know their drugs; they'll hammer them into their brains (with brute force if necessary!).

Moreover, over the past decade or so, the army of representatives has been expanding with particular vigor. For example, in the US alone, between 1996 and 2000, the herd of quacks with suitcases full of pills and ointments rose from an already impressive 41,800 to a fearsome 83,000 pharma-suits.

Yet, is this practice of "detailing" really effective? Hmm … (at best).

Research has shown, for example, that on average it takes three visits to induce one new prescription. It also takes an average of 26 additional free samples to generate one additional prescription. Hardly impressive, I'd say. Then why do most pharmaceutical companies continue to rely on detailing? Well, there are also studies – mostly internal research by the pharma companies themselves – that do not provide unambiguous evidence that detailing does not work. Hence, they're not 100 percent sure that it is an outdated practice. They fear there is a risk that if they stop using the practice they will lose money. And that's a risk they're not willing to take.

But, you might add, they're currently also at risk of losing money because they are continuing the practice. And you'd be right. However, we know from research – for example, on variations of "prospect theory", by Nobel Prize-winners Kahneman and Tversky – that people are often a lot more comfortable with the risk of losing money when everybody else is making the same mistake than with the risk of losing money when they'd be the odd one out (even if the latter amount is considerably less than the former).

For example, if a company were to stop detailing but it turned out they were wrong and they'd lose market share and money as a result of it, we (the public) would say, "You're stupid – nobody else did it". Currently, firms might be losing (a lot more) money because they continue detailing, but now none of us say they're stupid, because everybody is still doing it and we're just not sure that the practice is not effective. Hence, the risk of breaking the mold is perceived to be much higher than an undue acceptance of the status quo.

It is a situation very similar to that of the newspaper companies discussed earlier who were reluctant to switch to a tabloid-size format some years ago: they were just not sure that smaller newspapers would be popular. Hence, while everybody was printing broadsheet, nobody dared take the plunge and make the paper smaller.

> ❝ It takes someone to break the mold and show the way. ❞

It takes someone to break the mold and show the way. Usually, that is an outside entrant or a firm in financial distress (who just had to take a risk) – just like *The Independent* was in financial distress when it was the first to launch a small-size newspaper. Since those scenarios (outside entrants, financial distress) are unlikely in the world of pharma with its large entry barriers and deep pockets, detailing may be with us for quite a bit longer.

The Abilene paradox

Of course, it is not only firms that conform to what others are doing; individuals do too. For example, it is a well-known phenomenon from social psychology that people are reluctant to voice minority opinions. You may recognize this issue and have experienced it yourself sometimes; when a whole group of people seems to agree on something (a course of action, proposal, etc.) but you have doubts about it, it can be hard to speak up against it. And if you do collect the courage to speak up against it, you do so reluctantly, ready to take the heat.

And we're right to be reluctant to speak up. Research also shows that minority dissenters are often "punished", in the sense that people in the majority group get irritated, will blame you for the deal falling apart, may even start to give you the cold shoulder, if not spit in your tea when you're not looking.

Therefore, quite often, people don't speak up at all if they disagree with a particular course of action, if they feel they are likely to be the only ones against it. Instead, they stay quiet. And there is an interesting consequence to that. We only know that others disagree if they actually speak up. If they don't speak up, we are inclined to conclude that they do not disagree! As a result, it may be that we stay quiet because we assume that everybody else is in favor while, in reality, lots of others are making the same erroneous assumption! In social psychology, this phenomenon is known as pluralistic ignorance or the "Abilene paradox".

The first person to describe the Abilene paradox was Professor Jerry Harvey, from the George Washington University. He describes a leisure trip which he and his wife and parents made in Texas in July, in his parents' un-airconditioned old Buick to a town called Abilene. It was a trip they had all agreed to but, as it later turned out, none of them had wanted to go on. "Here we were, four reasonably sensible people who, of our own volition, had just taken a 106-mile trip across a godforsaken desert in a furnace-like temperature through a cloud-like dust storm to eat unpalatable food at a hole-in-the-wall cafeteria in Abilene, when none of us had really wanted to go!"

Of course, this phenomenon is not restricted to people in Texas. It happens in the world of business too. Professor Jim Westphal, from the University of Michigan, uncovered evidence of the Abilene paradox among boards of directors. He collected data on 228 boards of medium-sized American public companies using a variety of databases and questionnaires. He found out that outside directors often did not speak up against their company's extant strategy, even though they had serious concerns about it. At the same time, they greatly underestimated the extent to which their fellow directors shared these concerns! As a consequence, underperforming companies undertook fewer initiatives to change their strategy, and they persisted with their failing course of action.

That's the Abilene paradox. Nobody may think we're sailing a good course, but if nobody is willing to rock the boat – thinking we'll be the only one – we may end up continuing as is, until we all go under.

Same same but different

But that is not to say that we do not *like* being different, and doing something different. It is just a bit risky.

Normal people – you and I (well … at least you) – have an inclination to conform to certain peer groups, in the way we dress, speak, which music we like, how often we brush our teeth, buy a car, or go on a holiday. Yet, as normal people, on the other hand, we also like to stand out from the crowd (if just a little bit). It's known as "optimal distinctiveness theory".

66 We also like to stand out from the crowd. It's known as 'optimal distinctiveness theory'. 99

And sometimes CEOs are just like normal people.

Some years ago, I was working with an executive (who will remain blissfully anonymous) in charge of expanding his company into foreign markets, mainly through acquisitions. We analyzed his strategy and various market characteristics, through which it became obvious that the Scandinavian market, in his line of business, appeared to be particularly attractive. Yet, he clearly did not even want to think about entering this area. When I persisted in probing why, his answer was frank: "Look, none of my major competitors are active in that market, so there must be something wrong with it."

I was slightly stunned, but that was the end of it. Until, a few months later, I ran into him again. Having asked what he had been up to, he answered, "I've just entered the Scandinavian market". Upbeat, I asked him whether my advice had finally convinced him. His reply was, "Not exactly ... it is just that [my biggest competitor] has just entered the Scandinavian market, so it must be a good place after all."

I am not making this up, or even exaggerating (for a change). Was he unusual in this behavior? I think he was unusual in terms of the frankness of his admission, but not so much in terms of his behavior. As I said, one of the biggest influences on strategic decision-making – if not *the* biggest influence – is imitation. We do what others do around us. Academic research has indicated over and over again the prevalent nature of imitation among a wide array of management decisions, such as the adoption of conglomerates, choice of location when entering foreign markets, implementation of performance management programs (such as ISO 9000 or Six Sigma), product market entry, matrix organizations, and so on. Yet, like individuals in everyday life, CEOs don't like just doing what everybody else is doing; sometimes they just want to do something a bit different. For example, I recently analyzed a large database of about 800 companies in the pharmaceutical industry, focusing on the breadth of their product portfolio, and the statistical results clearly indicated that companies sometimes also choose to do the exact opposite of what their peers are doing, merely for the sake of doing something different.

Similarly, some time ago, I was working with several top executives of a British newspaper company, who faced the decision that I discussed earlier: whether or not to also adopt the new small-size paper format, just like several of their peers/competitors had. Ultimately, they decided against it. One of the executives said, "Had we been the first one to come up with the idea, we would have done it, but now that others have done it before us, we can't; it just wouldn't be very original." And in a way, I like this attitude. Granted, when you simply do the opposite of what others are doing, or explicitly do not want to do something just because your peers have done it, you're as much influenced by peer behavior as when you're an imitator (only 180 degrees opposite). Yet it also brings a bit more variety to the world, and hence makes life a bit more interesting. It gives you the opportunity, as a firm, to stand out from the crowd. And, who knows, perhaps even make an above-average profit as a result of it.

But, although we like being different, it is a difficult step to take, because it often also means that the outcome is uncertain. For example, if we wanted to go into the newspaper business in, say, 1990, we can get a pretty good idea what could happen if we used broadsheet paper; that market exists and is observable. But it is much harder to assess and compute what would happen if we entered with a tabloid-sized quality newspaper; that market did not yet exist and was therefore impossible to analyze or forecast. And we usually base our decisions on what we can see and analyze, and forget to pay attention to the things we cannot observe.

This relates to a broader, often overlooked, yet very prevalent and infuential phenomenon in the world of business and business decisions, and that is the stealthy danger of "selection bias".

"Selection bias"

During World War II, American military personnel noticed that some parts of planes seemed to be hit more often than other parts. They analyzed the bullet holes in the returning planes, and set out a program to have these areas reinforced, so that they would be better able to withstand enemy fire. This may seem natural enough, but it also contains a fundamental error: selection bias.

Assume, for the sake of the argument, that planes got hit in all sorts of places. If the areas which formed vital parts of the machine were hit (call it part A), the aeroplane was unlikely to make it back to base; it would crash. If bullets hit the plane in parts which were not so vital (part B), the plane was much more likely to make it back home. Then, military personnel would inspect the plane and conclude, "Darn, this plane also got hit in part B! We'd better strengthen those places ..."

Of course, the military personnel were wrong. Planes got hit in part A just as often as in part B; it's just that the former never made it back home. What's worse, strengthening part B was exactly the wrong thing to do: those parts weren't so vital; it is part A which needed strengthening!

This is why we call it "selection bias"; we only see a selection of the outcomes, and therefore draw false conclusions. And the world of business is full of this. Consider, for example, the popular notion that innovation projects require diverse, cross-functional teams. This notion exists because if we analyze some ground-breaking innovation projects, they were often staffed by such teams. However, Jerker Denrell from Oxford University suggested that diverse, cross-functional teams also often created the biggest failures of all! However, such failures never resulted in any products. Therefore, if we (only) examine the projects which actually resulted in successful innovations, it seems the diverse cross-functional teams did much better. Yet, on average, the homogeneous teams – although not responsible for the few really big inventions – might have done better, always producing a reliable, good set of results.

Similarly, we applaud CEOs who are bold and risk-taking, using their intuition rather than careful analysis, such as Jack Welch. However, risk, by definition, leads some to succeed but it also leads quite a few to fail, and slip into oblivion. Those CEOs we never consider; it is the risk-takers that happen to come out on top that we admire and aspire to. Yet, if we were able to see the full picture, of all CEOs, innovation teams, and fighter planes, we just might have reached a very different conclusion.

Numbers and strategy – do they mix?

There is a similar – and equally dangerous – bias in the world of business towards numbers; we pay a lot of attention to the things we can measure, calculate, and make "objective".

In your firm, when you come up with an idea for a new product line or service, or some other project that you think has great potential and want your company to invest in, what does management want to see? My guess is it's "payback time", a "net present value" calculation, or some other number in a business plan, right? And if you can't produce the numbers, you won't get the dosh. But that's also a bit of a problem; sometimes the most promising projects with long-term strategic implications are exactly those that are impossible to quantify.

66 sometimes the most promising projects with long-term strategic implications are exactly those that are impossible to quantify 99

Take Intel's invention of the microprocessor. In the early days, when they were working on and (quite heavily) investing in it, did they have a business plan, a net present value calculation and a payback time? Heck, no. They didn't even know what they were going to use them for – they had no sense of a potential application (dreaming of sticking them into handheld calculators and lamp-posts) till IBM showed up and worked hard to convince them that putting the darn things in their personal computers was the way to go.

Would microprocessors ever have seen the light of day in that firm if Intel's management had insisted on a "payback time" calculation? Nope, we'd still be using an abacus if they had insisted on seeing the numbers (OK, now I may be exaggerating) and Intel would never have been the mega-success it is now (not exaggerating).

So why do we insist on producing numbers if we're talking strategy? Genuine strategy, by definition, deals with long-term issues, uncertainty, and ambiguity. Hence, numbers don't work very well; they are unreliable, potentially misleading, and sometimes simply impossible to produce in such a situation. And I guess that is exactly why we/companies are so eager to see them. The long-term, uncertain aspects of strategic investment decisions make us insecure about whether we are doing the right thing; therefore, we really would like to see some numbers to lull ourselves into the belief that we've been thorough and have uncovered the facts and have a solid basis on which we're accepting or rejecting the proposed course of action. Of course that's just make-believe (you can make numbers say whatever you want them to say) and may make you myopic, missing the things that are difficult to quantify but just as important.

Am I proposing that we should get rid of numbers in strategy altogether? Heck, no; forcing yourself to go through some sort of quantifying exercise can sometimes make you uncover and realize things that you hadn't thought of before. But subsequently you should do what an (anonymous) CEO told me he always does when they've made financial calculations regarding new proposals: "Once we've carefully and painstakingly produced all the numbers, we toss them aside and sort of make a decision based on our gut feel and experience."

Numbers in strategy may form one (minor) input into your decision-making, but don't mistake them for the real thing: make the calculations, but then toss them aside and use your judgement and common sense.

Inebriated cyclists

Actually, business people's insistence on seeing the numbers always reminds me of the anecdote of the man looking for his keys under a lamp-post. A guy leaves a bar in the middle of the night. There, he sees a man on his hands and knees under a lamp-post, clearly looking for something. He asks him, "What are you looking for?" and the (slightly inebriated) man answers, "The keys to my bicycle; I must have lost them."

"I will help you look," says the guy, and on his hands and knees he starts to search too. After a good ten minutes have passed, still not having found the keys, he turns to the inebriated cyclist and says, "Are you sure you have lost them here? We've looked all over and they're nowhere to be found!"

"No," says the man, pointing towards a dark spot to the side of the road, "I lost them over there, but there it is so dark, I would never be able to find them."

The moral of this story is that we often look for solutions where there is light and we can see things, while the real cause of the problem lies in an area which is much more difficult to fathom.

Managers are often inebriated cyclists. If a company or division is in financial trouble, it cuts costs, slashes headcount, disinvests, sets stricter targets, and so on: the stuff that can be captured in numbers (i.e., "where it is light"), while the real cause of the problem will often be a lot more subtle, and lie in a tainted reputation, low employee morale, or low service quality. And looking hard where there's light won't make you discover the key to solving your problems any quicker. On the other hand, the hard stuff (which can be captured in numbers), such as production capacity, headcount, etc., are exactly the things that cannot give you much of a competitive advantage; they can often be bought off the shelf, meaning that your competitor can get it too. It's usually the soft stuff, such as morale, reputation, organizational culture, etc. (which we don't spend much time measuring, largely because these factors are difficult to observe and capture in numbers) that can make all the difference, because they can't be bought, and take much time and effort to develop.

Hence, don't be misled by the hard stuff, which you can measure; of course you need it but it will seldom give you a competitive advantage or get you out of trouble. The soft things, which we cannot see and measure, are the ones that you have to carefully nurture and manage.

Deciding stuff – that's the easy bit

This reliance on numbers and analysis also points at two different views of what top managers do, or perhaps two aspects of their daily jobs:

1 Decision-makers (investment decisions, acquisitions, which markets to enter, and so forth)
2 People who have to build and manage a firm.

Of course, the two overlap, but they are also different.

Some time ago, my friend and colleague at the London Business School, Phanish Puranam, and I ran a short (unpublished) survey with 111 top managers, all alumni from our School's senior executive program. We gave them a list of 35 strategic management topics, asking them to rate each of them on a seven-point scale, ranging from unimportant to very important for corporate leaders in today's business environment.

The three things that these senior executives said were the most important issues in their view and experience were:

1 Attract and retain talent
2 Decide on the company's next avenues of growth
3 Align the organization towards one common goal.

Some further (statistical) analysis showed us that the most important issue, "attract and retain talent", pertained to things such as putting together an effective top management team, and managing top management succession. Many business leaders see their main task as recruiting and developing other leaders, and it seems our senior executives were no exception.

The second one – "decide on the company's next avenues of growth" – reminded me of a survey a famous global consulting firm used to run. It ran an annual survey asking CEOs, "What keeps you awake at night?" It was one of these PR endeavors aimed at getting some free publicity in the business press, bolstering their image as a source of management knowledge and wisdom. However, this survey was not a great success, and they stopped running it, simply because every year the same thing came out on top (which made it rather boring and hardly ideal to get the business press excited ...) and that was: "The firm's next avenue of growth". Our survey confirmed this result.

The third one – "align the organization towards one common goal" – pertained to something that tends to make non-senior executives (including business school professors) smirk: creating a mission and vision statement. These vision thingies inevitably seem to lead to some generic yet draconian expressions (e.g., "to be the pre-eminent" something) that could only be generated by a de-generated consultant brain. Moreover, inevitably they appear to be highly similar to the terminology on the wall of the firm next door. Nevertheless, our senior executives do seem to take them seriously. I guess they're typical of top managers' struggle to "align the organization towards one common goal"; in their desperation they even turn to hammering a mission or vision statement on the canteen's wall. Guess it really is a struggle.

What struck me about these three topics, however, is that none of them are *decisions*. It seems – also from analyzing the remainder of our survey – that top managers are unfazed by strategic decisions, no matter how big and far-reaching they are. But things they can't "decree" – like having an effective team, organic growth, or a common vision – are what keep them awake.

Indeed, you can't just declare, "I decide that next year our organic growth will be 30 percent." Instead, you will have to build and nurture an organization that fosters innovation and motivates people and other stakeholders to achieve autonomous growth. You can't just decide to have it, like you decide to pursue a particular acquisition, enter a new foreign market, or diversify into a new line of business. Similarly, you can't just decide to attract and retain talent, or decide that "from now on everybody will believe in the same vision and aspiration". It simply doesn't work that way. And apparently top managers are a lot more comfortable with stuff they can decide than with things that are not under their direct control: things they need to foster and carefully build up over a longer period of time. And I don't blame them: that stuff is easier said than done.

How well do you know your company? (My guess is not very well at all ...)

So far, I have been explaining that in many companies and decision-making processes there is a bias towards the things that we can observe and measure. Numbers give us a (false) sense of security, that we are objective and in control of the process. However, how accurate are managers' observations, and how well do they generally know the numbers they so often talk about? Let me give you a few examples.

In the 1970s, there was a series of academic studies which looked at managers' perceptions of the "volatility" of their company's business environments. These studies all found that different managers within the same organization had widely varying views on how volatile their business was: the correlation between different people's assessments was virtually zero. In addition, these studies found that there was hardly any relation between objective measures of business volatility and managers' estimates of these measures (if anything, the correlations were negative; managers in stable environments thought their business was relatively turbulent, and vice versa). Similar results were obtained for other variables. The researchers concluded that managers' perceptions of their own businesses were usually plain wrong.

Two business school professors, John Mezias and Bill Starbuck, at the time at New York University, set out to examine this claim further (and published their results a few years ago) simply because they found it hard to believe, at least at first. They thought "'business volatility', that's a bit vague and abstract, let's start with something simple" and they asked executives from a wide range of companies to tell them their business unit's sales for the previous year. Then they looked up the units' actual sales figures. The average answer was 475.7 percent wrong. That's 475.5 percent ...! Sales of their own business unit!!

Then John and Bill thought, "Perhaps we should pick something they find really important". So they approached a blue-chip company and asked it what the company's absolute top-notch priority was: the CEO declared that the absolute top priority throughout the entire company was "quality improvement".

And indeed, that seemed to be true: many managers attended quality improvement training courses, each division had a dedicated department focusing on quality performance, and the company had developed various quality metrics. Furthermore, all managers received quarterly quality improvement reports, and 74 percent of them indicated in a survey that they expected to receive large increases in their personal rewards if their divisions managed to increase quality. Yep, "quality" was important to them!

Quality was measured in the company, following the specialist training techniques, in terms of "sigma" (a measurement of the error rate in their production output). When John and Bill asked the managers what the sigma of their department was, the average error in their answer was ... (wait for it) ... 715.1 percent. A whopping 715 percent! They really had no clue.

Note that these had been managers brave enough to give any answer at all; 7 out of 10 managers, when asked, had refused to give any estimate, declaring, "I don't know". It seems likely that they had realized they had no clue, and rather than make a complete fool of themselves, they opted not to say anything.

Granted, when John and Bill finally asked the brave ones who dared to give an answer to express their unit's error rate not in terms of the illustrious "sigma" but in plain human terms of "What percentage of products have errors?" they did a lot better: almost 7 out of 10 managers managed to give an answer which was less than 50 percent off the mark.

Of course these people are not all fools. They are usually smart, well-trained, and hard-working. It is just that they have no clue about the numbers describing their own business – and managers usually don't. We spend a lot of time, money, effort, and attention quantifying all sorts of aspects of our organizations but, at the end of the day, make decisions ignoring all these numbers, using instead our experience, qualitative assessment, and gut instinct. And that's probably for the better; if we based decisions on our (alleged) knowledge of the numbers, we'd be prone to shoot ourselves not only in the foot, but also in the chin, the head, the backside, and the bodily parts of several of our neighbors.

How to make a compelling corporate strategy in six easy steps

Numbers and analysis seem to form part of the corporate façade of structured decision-making. However, over the years, my observations of how the strategy process in corporations is usually organized is quite different. It usually seems to consist of six consecutive steps.

Step 1: On October 15th (or whatever day and month), we send a memo to our business unit managing directors that we will need their unit's strategy input by December 1st, including an explicit elaboration of how it fits in with the corporation's overall strategy.

Step 2: BU's management thinks, "What was the corporate strategy again?" and looks up last year's document.

Step 3: It takes note of what its business unit's input needs to be – in terms of the guidelines provided by corporate – and, after a week or so, assigns some junior staff members, consultants, or interns to provide the numbers about the market, forecasts, benchmarking (in terms of what competitors are doing), and so on. They give them last year's document and also send round an e-mail to all team leaders urging them to provide the necessary data ("because it is that time of year again" and corporate wants it by December 1st).

Step 4: After two weeks, BU management thinks, "Wonder how that is going?" and finds out that the team leaders have been slow to provide the necessary information. After another e-mail (marked "urgent"), information starts flowing in and by mid-November there is a big pile of data. In the subsequent two weeks (while flipping through last year's documents a bit), they write a number of pages about what the unit has been doing over the past year (which corresponds remarkably well with what they said last year they would be doing), what they will be doing next year and how it is all contributing to (yes, even driven by!) the overall corporate strategy. On December 1st, we note from our e-mail inbox that we received their document last night on November 30th (just in time!), at 11:37pm, which makes us realize, with a slight feeling of guilt, that we had just gone to bed at that time (after finishing a rather good bottle of Australian shiraz).

Step 5: The next day, we flip through the various units' strategy documents and put them aside. Some time during the first week of January, we flip through them again and take last year's corporate strategy document out of the drawer. We then think about all the activities the corporation is engaged in and – usually with the aid of our strategy department or, in the blissful absence of such a group, a consultant or two (they usually hunt in packs) – we come up with some overarching logic (and a quite compelling one, we proudly congratulate ourselves) of why we are doing the various things we're doing anyway.

Step 6: On February 1st, we send the document to all company directors and business unit managing directors. They look at its shiny cover (with a picture of us standing in front of our new corporate building

– we first objected to having our own picture on the cover, but PR convinced us it would give it a more personal touch), read the first page (checking the acknowledgements for their name), briefly flip through some of the other chapters, and put it in a drawer. Where it remains until October 15th, when we remind them, "It is that time of year again".

DAVE CARPENTER..

" I THINK WE SHOULD IMMEDIATELY LAUNCH THIS PROGRAM BEFORE OUR COMMON SENSE SETS IN. "

Previously published in Harvard Business Review, March 2002

Wanna play Strategy? Get a board game

OK, I might have exaggerated a bit above, but not too much (and only to make a point)! Certainly not more than the people who pretend that strategizing in their firm is a rational, systematic, and objective process. As a matter of fact, it continues to surprise me what people sometimes proclaim is their business strategy. Take for instance the principles I often hear people suggest form the basis of their acquisition strategy.

When a particular transaction is being considered, executives have to go out and explain the logic behind the deal to directors, investors, and analysts. Regularly, however, a strategic rationale is only drawn up after it has been decided by management that the deal is "desirable". Quite often, this logic will appear contrived, overly complex, or simply made to fit the acquisition rather than the deal resulting from a well thought-through strategy in the first place.

For example, I've often heard the logic behind a transaction being explained in terms of complementarities; "It is a perfect match because their geographic spread perfectly matches ours" or, "Their product portfolio complements ours", and so forth. Yet, just as often I would hear the logic being explained exactly the other way around; in terms of perfect overlap, for instance, "It is a perfect match because they are active in the exact same markets as we are."

Just the fact that you "complement" each other does not constitute a strategy. It might be worthwhile to combine forces, but first you'd need an argument to explain why this would enable you to create extra value. Without such logic, it's hollow and meaningless. Similarly, just because you have perfect overlap doesn't automatically imply it's a good strategy. Why does adding it up enable you to do something you could not do before?

Yet, the one that always gets me is "the matrix". Yep, really a matrix. On the horizontal axis, one places countries (in which the company is active). On the vertical axis, one places business lines (in which the company is active). Then, on the intersections, one ticks boxes (with a decisive "X") indicating in which countries we have which line of business. And our strategy is: We fill the boxes. As many as possible.

"This acquisition is expensive, but it enables us to immediately tick six boxes!" Wow, yes, surely this warrants an 80 percent takeover premium – well done indeed; six boxes! We're doing well, aren't we?"

I agree strategy is simple, but it's not *that* simple!

Because strategy is really not the same as a game of Risk, placing pawns on a map of the world. Sure, perhaps it can be advantageous to own multiple business lines in that particular set of countries, but without a thorough explanation of why these countries (and not others), and these lines of business (and not others), and why it is beneficial to have them all, that's what it is; an oversized game of Risk, but with real money, and real people.

"Framing contests": what really happens in strategy meetings

So, if strategy development is usually not a rational, structured process, in which options are developed, analyzed, and decided upon, what does happen in strategy-making meetings?

One of the first series of strategy-making meetings I ever attended was in a large newspaper company. I was basically a fly on the wall, watching the process unfold with a mixture of curiosity, puzzlement, and amazement, like a Martian watching a cricket game (or so I imagine). It quickly struck me that there seemed to be a number of pre-formed sub-groups, with their own opinions and agenda. You had the people who wanted to take the company public, those who thought they should diversify into other areas of business, those who thought they should become a "green company", and so on, and those who thought they shouldn't care out of a matter of principle.

Of course there were some political motives at play, but mostly these people seemed genuinely convinced that their opinion was what was best for the future of the company. And, rather than coming up with new ideas, the strategy meetings seemed to consist of the various people trying to convince each other to believe in their view of the company, its future, and the changes required.

Many years later, I read the PhD dissertation of Sarah Kaplan, a former McKinsey consultant turned Professor at the Wharton Business School. Sarah described such strategy meetings as "framing contests". Framing contests, she said, concern "the way actors attempt to transform their personal cognitive frames into predominant collective frames through a series of interactions in the organization". And although I had to read that sentence a couple of times (before I endeavored to even begin to believe that I had any clue what the heck she was talking about) it gradually struck me as quite accurate.

In strategy meetings, people try to convince each other by painting a mental image of the future: what would happen if they continued as they were, and what could happen if they followed the course of action proposed by them. They might throw in some numbers based on "research" (put together long after they had made up their mind), and engage in spirited debate, complete with raised voices, rolling eyes, and the occasional hand gesture.

And you would win the contest if, through a series of debates, you managed to convince others and get your view of the company and its future adopted as the dominant frame, defining how the organization sees itself and what it is trying to achieve in the market.

And this may not be a bad way of doing things. I saw the same process unfold – quite successfully – in model-train maker Hornby, where the debate centered on divesting, diversifying, investing more, or outsourcing production to China (the latter faction won). Similarly, it famously led Intel, over the course of several years, to abandon its memory business in favor of microprocessors.

Former Intel chief executive Andy Grove said about this: "The faction representing the x86 microprocessor business won the debate, even though the 386 had not yet become the big revenue generator that it eventually would become."

Stanford professor Robert Burgelman (who spent a lifetime studying Intel), wrote about this same episode: "Some managers sensed that the existing organizational strategy was no longer adequate and that there were competing views about what the new organizational strategy should be. Top management as a group, it seems, was watching how the organization sorted out the conflicting views."

Later, Andy Grove concurred that that is what happened, and quite deliberately so: "You dance around it a bit, until a wider and wider group in the company becomes clear about it. That's why continued argument is important. Intel is a very open system. No one is ever told to shut up, but you are asked to come up with better arguments."

So, next time you find yourself debating your company's strategy and future, realize you're in a framing contest. What you will need most are not ideas but powers of persuasion. And that is what you will need the numbers, analysis, and PowerPoint presentations for. Not to make up your mind (you probably already have) but as a hammer, a mace, and a club; those are the tools you require when you want to win a framing contest.

It looks like we don't have a strategy ...

But let me, at the end of this first chapter, not leave you with the impression that it is all bad. Actually, I am almost inclined to suggest that *especially* successful and innovative business strategies did not usually emerge through some rational, top-down process. I have no formal proof of this, but it is certainly the impression I have gained from studying many companies and their strategies.

Whenever I interview people at a particular company regarding their firm's strategy – for instance, because I am writing a business case about them – I try to make a point of finding out not only exactly what their strategy is, and why it works, but also where it came from. That is, how they came up with the strategy in the first place. And usually, I get a perfectly logical and rational answer – at least at first ... However, often, when I subsequently dig deeper into the organization, by interviewing middle managers and engineers (who have been there for a long time), by talking to the CEO again, by reading up on some internal company documentation, and so on, it appears that the (wonderful) strategy was not the result of rational analysis at all. Instead, invariably, it seems, there was some lucky moment or unexpected event that triggered the company to alter its course and move in a new direction.

Hornby accidentally saw itself appear in the hobby market (instead of the toy market) when it spent its cost savings from outsourcing on adding detail and quality to its products; CNN figured out it could become a global (instead of an American) news company when Fidel Castro (picking up the American satellite signal in Havana) told founder Ted Turner he watched it all the time; Southwest invented low-cost airlines when competition forced it to sell a plane but it decided to try and fly the same routes with three instead of four aircraft; and Bisque founder Geoffrey Ward switched from being a plumber to selling designer radiators when people kept knocking on his door asking whether they could buy that funny-shaped radiator which he had just removed for a client and placed in his workshop window to make it look like a shop (to see off the civil servants who had told him he was illegally located in a retail zone).

But why do people, in retrospect, always want to make it sound like it was the result of some thorough analysis and innovative thinking? Ego? Embarrassment? I guess that might play a role: "rational thinking" sounds better than "ehm … we stumbled upon it, I guess …" But, I've also found that people I interviewed who weren't even there at the time of the strategic switch – and therefore can't take any credit or blame for it – make it sound logical. And that is, I guess, because in retrospect, it all sounds so bloody obvious: moving into the hobby market, becoming global, not handing out food, newspapers, and hot towels on a 45-minute flight (but instead focusing on turning the darn thing around on the tarmac in 20 minutes and ready to fly again). It just makes so much sense that it just had to be the result of thorough analysis and thinking – surely?

❝ the best strategies often emerge when you least expect them to ❞

But admitting, even if just to yourself, that the best strategies often emerge when you least expect them to, could actually help you get lucky more often. Andy Grove, former CEO and chairman of Intel, figured that one out when Intel moved its microprocessors into computers after IBM (finally) convinced Intel that they could be applied in their PCs and, yes, they really wanted to buy them. After that, he said: "We say we have a top-to-bottom strategy. But [we] don't act top-to-bottom. You can look at it positively or negatively. Positively, it looks like a Darwinian process: we let the best ideas win; we match evolving skills with evolving opportunities. Negatively, it looks like we don't have a strategy."

And you want to make sure ideas reach you from everywhere: suppliers, customers, competitors, bloody civil servants and, yes, even Fidel Castro.

2

The success trap (and some ideas how to get out of it)

Why good companies go bad

Did you know that when you take the list of Fortune 100 companies in 1966 (America's largest companies) and compare it with the Fortune 100 in 2006, 66 of those companies don't even exist anymore? Another 15 still exist but don't feature on the list any longer, while a mere 19 of them are still there.

It pertains to this phenomenon we call the the "success trap"; ample research and statistics show, for a variety of industries, that very successful firms have trouble staying successful and adapting to fundamental changes in their business environments (such as new competitors, different customer demand, radical new technologies, or business models, and so forth). Over the years, they have focused on the thing that made them successful (a particular product, service, production method, etc.) and as a result became even better at it. Yet, this came at the expense of other products, processes, and viewpoints, which were considered much less important and were often discarded. Hence, the company had become very good at one thing, but one thing only. This is not a problem unless, of course, your environment changes. It's just that most environments have the nasty habit of doing exactly that ...

Then, the company is caught off-guard, and has trouble adapting to the altered circumstances. It is partly a cognitive thing. For example, how come that, in the early 1980s, IBM so dramatically misunderstood the emergence of personal computers? How come Harley-Davidson was all but wiped out of the market by tiny Japanese entrants like Honda, who made very different motorcycles? How come the once dominant Firestone completely misread the emergence of radial tires and went down the drain? Laura Ashley, Atari, Digital Equipment, Tupperware, Revlon: the list goes on and on of once dominant companies that at some point seem to lose the plot and get into severe trouble.

Some of them recover, some of them go under, arrogantly assuming that what they always had been doing – and what had brought them so much success – would always work, only to find out, the hard way, and often too late, that they were wrong, and the world did not need them any longer.

Where in the first chapter of this book I told you about the various determinants of many big business decisions, in this chapter I want to zoom in to one specific yet very influential one: success. The experience of success is a huge determinant of many a firm's subsequent chosen course of action. But, as the success trap illustrates, it is not always a positive one. Here I'll expose what happens in organizations that fall into the success trap. I'd also like to tell you about creosote bushes, give you the analogy of a major operation in World War II, and share some insights from a Nobel Prize-winning line of experiments.

In the second part of the chapter, I use these insights to explain what companies may be able to do to escape a crisis, whether the crisis is limited to the organization itself, its industry, or when it concerns a global downturn. I want to tackle the harrowing yet pivotal question, "Is your company brave enough to survive?"

The Icarus paradox

The success trap is also known as the "Icarus paradox" in business. Icarus was a figure in Greek mythology. Together with his father, Daedalus, he was held prisoner in a labyrinth, so obviously had trouble getting out (after all, it was a labyrinth!). And when they finally managed to find their way out, they found themselves stuck on an island. Then, Daedalus had a bright idea. He started collecting feathers that had dropped from the sky (I can only assume from over-flying birds, but anything can happen in Greek mythology) and glued them onto some twigs using beeswax. He made two pairs of wings.

And he told his son, "Icarus, let's fly out of here!" Initially, Icarus thought, "Yeah old guy, like that's going to work; a pair of wings!" But Daedalus said, "Believe me son, they will work, just try them". And Icarus did. He put on the wings and, cautiously, started flapping his arms. Much to his surprise, he took off!

Icarus was flying, initially quite cautiously but gradually he grew more confident and started to enjoy his flight. He started flying higher and higher. His father, Daedalus, shouted, "Don't go too high!" but Icarus didn't hear him (or, more likely for an adolescent, ignored him) and went even higher. Until he started flying too close to the sun … The beeswax melted, the feathers popped out, and Icarus fell to earth: dead (the Greeks are no wimps in their mythology).

This is why we call it the Icarus *paradox*; the same thing that had made him successful, that had helped him escape the prison and fly, is what led to his downfall. In his overconfidence he had become blind to the dangers of flying too close to the sun.

And this is what we often see very successful companies do too; they become very good and successful doing one particular thing, but this also makes them overconfident and blind to the dangers that new developments in their business pose to them, which ultimately may lead to their downfall.

But what causes it? There are various parts to the explanation but one of them pertains to how the top managers of those very successful companies perceive the changes in their business environment. In a way, it is good old tunnel vision, for example in terms of how top managers interpret the changes in their business environment.

Tunnel vision – "in the end, there is only flux"

"Tunnel vision is caused by an optic fungus that multiplies when the brain is less energetic than the ego. It is complicated by exposure to politics. When a good idea is run through the filters and compressors of ordinary tunnel vision, it not only comes out reduced in scale and value but in its new dogmatic configuration produces effects the opposite of those for which it originally was intended." Tom Robbins, in *Still Life with Woodpecker.*

Research by Professors Allen Amason from the University of Georgia and Ann Mooney from the Stevens Institute of Technology, for example, has shown that CEOs of firms with relatively high performance were significantly more likely to interpret changes in their business environment as a threat than CEOs of poorly performing companies, who more often interpreted changes as a positive thing.

And this is understandable. If you are the top performer in your industry, any change looks like a threat, because things can only get worse; you like things just the way they are, thank you very much! In contrast, if you currently look like a sucker because you're the CEO of a company that is not performing very well in comparison to your peers, any change is welcome. It represents an opportunity for things to be altered, and your only way is up.

Allen and Ann also showed that, as a consequence, the top managers of the high-performing companies were much less comprehensive in formulating a response to the strategic change; they didn't spend much time evaluating potential alternative courses of action, they didn't do much research and analysis, and they sure as hell didn't seek any outside help or opinion.

Most likely, executives in such a situation are going to try to continue as is, resist change or minimize its impact. However, if the environmental change is profound, ignoring it is likely not going to work! And this is a problem of all times. In the 1970s, the Swiss watch industry, which was superb at making mechanical watches, invented the quartz watch but they didn't do anything with it. And when companies from Hong Kong and Japan flooded the market with cheap quartz watches they denied the relevance of the change till they had a near-death experience.

Around the same time, tire-maker Firestone responded to the introduction of radial technology by trying to beef up its production of bias tires (their financials continued to plunge until they were put out of misery and acquired by competitor Bridgestone). More recently, traditional newspaper companies fought news-reporting on the Internet by suing dot-coms and naïvely copying and pasting their own paper on a website, while Kodak for a long time tried to ignore digital photography, mourning its spectacular margins on photo-film.

> ❝ When your company is hugely successful, you don't want to see that the world is changing. ❞

I guess that's why you could call it old-fashioned tunnel vision. When your company is hugely successful, you don't want to see that the world is changing. And if you then, eventually, are forced to incorporate the new technology (or whatever it is that is rocking your world), you try to squeeze it into your own version of reality, rather than accept that reality itself has changed. But reality is that one day the likes of industry giants like Google, Intel, or Microsoft will go down. Because as Heraclitus already said some five centuries BC: "panta rhei" (everything flows); and "In the end, there is only flux, everything gives way".

❝ In the end, there is only flux, everything gives way. ❞

Tunnel vision is of course not only restricted to organizations in the world of business. One pertinent example, I have always thought, concerned Operation Market Garden, an operation by the Allied forces during World War II.

Operation Market Garden

My father was a young boy during World War II. He grew up in a small village in the Netherlands just south of the river Maas which, parallel to two arms of the river Rhine, flows from east to west, cutting the country in half. In 1944, while the Allied forces were moving north, approaching the Netherlands from Belgium after having landed in Normandy, the barn behind his home served as a makeshift German army hospital, while their commanders took up headquarters in the family's living room. When the German soldiers left, the barn filled up with wounded Allied soldiers instead, and the German commanders at his dinner table were replaced by their English-speaking counterparts.

He never told me about what he saw in the barn. He did recall with fondness the sweets and cigarettes the soldiers used to give him (he was 10 years old), Germans and Americans alike. Anyway, he used to tell me about the operations that the Allied forces conducted to get across the big rivers, trying to advance into the north of the Netherlands. One of them was Operation Market Garden. It was a huge operation, involving some 35,000 troops, in which soldiers, weaponry, vehicles, and equipment were dropped near bridges crossing the three rivers, to occupy and hold them while the Allied forces advanced through the south of the Netherlands, preventing the German troops from blowing them up.

Years later, I saw the (apparently very accurate) film *A Bridge too Far*, starring Dirk Bogarde, James Caan, Michael Caine, Robert Redford, Sean Connery, and Anthony Hopkins; clearly, a 1970s' star cast.

I had become a professional student of organizations by then, having accepted a position as an assistant Professor of Strategy at the London Business School. It was then that I was struck by the similarities between the processes that lead up to spectacular business failures and the processes that made Operation Market Garden a disaster.

Because Operation Market Garden was a huge failure. It became one of the biggest massacres of the whole war; more people died in Operation Market Garden than on D-Day itself. The Allied forces did not manage to hold the third bridge at Arnhem, and it took another eight months before the north of the Netherlands was liberated; during the preceding winter, thousands of people, cut off from the agricultural lands of the south, perished in a famine known as "the hungerwinter".

Yet, the commanders in charge of the operation had received many early warning signs that it was going to be a challenge: perhaps a bridge too far. The Dutch Resistance had sent coded messages that at least one German tank division was located unexpectedly close to the Allied forces' drop zone (their warnings were ignored); English spy-plane pictures examining the drop zones had taken photographs of the tanks (the photographs were brushed aside); officers and a general had expressed doubts about the preparations for the operation (their hesitations were dismissed); and soldiers questioned whether the radios, to be used for vital co-ordination and communication on the ground, would work (they didn't).

So why did the general in charge of the operation (General Browning) ignore all these warning signs? Well, for the same reasons as top executives go ahead with a big acquisition despite due diligence suggesting it's a bad idea, and why companies go ahead with a planned product launch despite retailers and salespeople warning the product isn't ready yet: we call it "escalation of commitment". There is a lot riding on the project, both in terms what is at stake (the future of the company; the war) and in terms of the personal reputation of the person in charge. Pulling the plug will make you look stupid and incompetent; succeeding will make you a hero. And you have made a very public commitment to seeing the project through, having championed it from the start. There is no way of stopping it now.

And when you plan an operation of this size, whether it is Operation Market Garden or a huge acquisition, nothing is ever going to be perfect. If you pull the plug each time something is amiss, you're never going to achieve anything; you need a high level of commitment and persistence in the presence of setbacks.

❝ The trick is knowing when to pull the plug – It's a judgment call. ❞

However, at some point, your commitment is going to escalate: it's going to be too much, and the warning signs are going to be ubiquitous. The trick is knowing when to pull the plug – and unfortunately it's not like you can put that in a spreadsheet, hit Enter and see the answer. It's a judgment call.

And being too late to make this call, realize it is has become too much, and you're going to have to bite the bullet and admit the error of your ways is, I am afraid, only human. Yet the consequences can be disastrous, and truly a bridge too far.

Mental models – let's all think within the same box

What makes the related phenomena of the success trap, tunnel vision, and escalation of commitment so tricky is that it is the same things that lead to success that may also get you in trouble. For example, one does often need some pigheadedness to succeed, and carry on where others would have stopped. Yet, obviously this can go too far, and lead to failure. It is largely a mental thing, and one that applies to individuals and businesses alike.

The illustrious former chairman of IBM, Thomas Watson, once said, "Whenever an individual or a business decides that success has been attained, progress stops." What he meant was that successful firms find it very hard to change, for instance in response to changes in their business environment. (Unfortunately he is also the person who allegedly said, "I think there is a world market for maybe five computers" so I would say, "Physician heal thyself" … but I guess that doesn't make him wrong about the first bit!)

As said, this rigidity-due-to-success effect is partly a mental thing. Once something has brought us success for a sustained period of time, we sort of forget that there are other ways of doing things. It may even be so bad that we don't spot the changes in our business environment at all anymore. However, let's not make the mistake of thinking that such strong mental models of how we go about doing our business are all bad. They also bring some pretty strong advantages. Consider the following:

Aoccdrnig to rscheearch at an Elingsh uinervtisy, it deosn't mttaer in waht oredr the ltteers in a wrod are, the olny iprmoetnt tihng is taht the frist and the lsat ltteer are at the rghit pclae. The rset can be a toatl mses and you can sitll raed it wouthit a porbelm. Tihs is bcuseae we do not raed ervey lteter by itslef but the wrod as a wlohe.

All of the above is clearly nonsense; they're not words at all, it is just gibberish. But something makes us able to read it without a problem; that's because all the right pieces of information are there (all the letters) and roughly in the right shape. Plus, the context (the sentence) makes sense to us. Then, our brain does the rest. We can understand it precisely because we have seen the individual elements (the words) before and understand the context.

It is the same in business situations; we can quickly grasp and interpret a particular issue if we understand the context and have seen similar problems and situations before. We don't have to reinvent the wheel every time we see a similar problem, but can build on our experience. Thus, forming mental models is how we learn; they enable us to make quick decisions without the need for complete information. This is a powerful thing to have for every organization. You don't want everyone thinking outside the box all the time; a coherent group of like-minded people with lots of common experience can be a very useful asset indeed.

The negative effects of common mental models – blindness to changes and viewpoints that don't fit the model, something known as "groupthink" – you can possibly overcome through smart organizational design. For example, I've seen large organizations that created multiple similar sub-units: each of them coherent, but also very different from each other. They attempt to get the best of both worlds: coherence within units, diversity between them.

❝ groupthink can be a good thing, as long as you have multiple groups … ❞

Hence, groupthink can be a good thing, as long as you have multiple groups …

A creosote bush: how "exploitation" drives out "exploration"

The tension between creating an organization that is highly focused, reaping the profits of what it is good at, and one which steps outside the box and creates new sources of growth and revenue is one that many companies struggle with. It is probably also *the* one thing that pretty much every CEO that I talk to recognizes, regards as a pivotal issue, and a genuine and continuing struggle. That is because established, very profitable companies almost invariably find it difficult to remain innovative (which may get them into trouble in the long run). In contrast, entrepreneurial, innovative companies often find it difficult to start producing efficiently and make a healthy profit out of their inventions. That is because the type of organization required to be creative and innovative is quite different from an organization that is suited for efficient, mass-scale production.

Professor Jim March from the Stanford Business School eloquently put it like this: he said there is a fundamental tension between "exploitation and exploration". Exploration involves innovation and creativity, which often requires a high level of autonomy for people in the organization and a flat organizational structure. Exploitation is associated with words such as productivity, efficiency, and control, which require hierarchy and clear rules and procedures.

If a company is financially successful, exploitation often starts to crowd out exploration. This relates to the idea of the "success trap": organizations start to focus more and more on what they do well, the thing that brings them success and prosperity. Yet this comes at the expense of other things, which may not be so profitable now but which could (have) become important for the firm in the long run.

Even the famous Intel fell into this trap. In the 1980s and 1990s, Intel had become hugely successful in the microprocessor business by being extremely innovative and running many experiments in semiconductors. Yet, once they had developed an enormous advantage in microprocessors, they gradually stopped doing anything else. In 1996, CEO Andy Grove recognized the long-term dangers of this and remarked, "There is a hidden danger of Intel becoming very good at this. It is that we become good at one thing." Yet he also found himself unable to revive Intel's entrepreneurial creativity.

In 1993 microprocessors made up 75 percent of Intel's revenues and 85 percent of its profits. By 1998, this had increased to 80 percent of its revenues but 100 percent of its profits! This mega-company basically had only one product, on which they relied to bring in all the dosh. If you think that sounds a bit risky, I agree with you. The company's COO Craig Barrett remarked about this that Intel's core microprocessor business "had begun to resemble a creosote bush". In case you're not a botanist (and, like me, only appreciate plants when they come on a dinner plate), a creosote bush is a desert plant that survives by poisoning the ground around it, so that nothing else can grow in its vicinity ... Quite a peculiar way to qualify your top-selling product, I'd say, but not a bad analogy. Microprocessors were so successful that no other product could grow within Intel, because it would always look bad in comparison to these darn processor things.

Of all the organizations that I have studied over the past decade and a half, the one that has probably impressed me most in this respect is the famous Sadler's Wells theater in London. On the one hand, it is phenomenally innovative, putting on the most novel and creative modern dance shows on the planet. But, on the other hand, it also stages a substantial number of shows that are tried and tested, and from which it knows that it will reap a healthy profit.

How does it maintain this balance so well? There are several complementary explanations, but one of them is that the theater works on it continuously, literally every day. It aims for about 15–30 percent of totally new innovative shows in the program (often the result of a collaboration between artists who usually wouldn't work together, because they have very different styles, background, or training) and discuss this issue all the time. They do that in regular formal meetings, which invariably involve people from various departments, but also on an ongoing informal basis (that is, in the corridors, in the restaurant, and in the restroom).

They are always discussing which show should go where on the theater's calendar, for how long it should be scheduled, what other show needs to be scheduled around the same time, etc. Because they continuously discuss and work on it, they manage to get the balance right. And, as their numbers show, the cool thing is that often, those shows which at the time were exploratory and considered risky and innovative, are now the ones that contribute most to their bank account.

A bitter pill

Consider, in contrast, the pharmaceutical industry. It was always hard to think of a nicer business to be in than pharmaceuticals. Think about it, how much more price-insensitive can customers be? In many countries, due to medical insurance, the people deciding on what product to purchase (i.e., doctors) are not the ones paying for it, nor are the people who are actually swallowing the pill! And what if these consumers were responsible for payment, what are they going to say, "Are you kidding, $30 for that pill is really overpriced; I'd rather die!" Well, that's the problem, you just might ...

Moreover, there are not many substitutes available for chemical drugs; acupuncture and an occasional mud-bath and that's about it. Furthermore, the suppliers of the pharma companies are hardly able to squeeze profit out of them, as the raw materials are usually bulk commodities. On top of that, the entry barriers into the industry are huge, among others due to lengthy product development times and enormous upfront financial investments required (about $800 million for an average new drug).

Best of all though, is that demand is virtually unlimited! It's not as if we will run out of diseases to cure. Many drugs have such severe side-effects that we need other drugs to suppress them! A cycle as virtuous as I have ever seen. Yep, pharmaceuticals was a nice place to be in.

But lately, pharmaceutical companies have been showing signs of distress. This distress is relative – because they're still making money by the bucket – but once you're used to a Gucci life it is not easy to downgrade to the Gap. One reason for this distress is the fact that for many companies, product pipelines have all but dried up; R&D departments are just not coming up with the goodies.

There may be various reasons for this, but it is quite clear from academic research that innovation becomes more difficult when you're old and rich. For example, Professor Henrich Greve, currently at INSEAD Business School, examining Japanese shipbuilders over a period of several decades, found that firms with deep pockets invested quite a bit more in R&D but, concurrently, also launched fewer new products. Professors Jesper Sørensen and Toby Stuart, at the time both at the University of Chicago, examining firms in biotech and in semiconductors, found that older firms came up with more innovations but that these were usually less influential and concerned mere variations on already well-known themes.

The problem for top managers is that a lack of innovation is not solved by money alone. Top managers can decide many things; as discussed in Chapter 1, they can decide to acquire company X, throw in money and a team of bankers and see it done. They can decide to enter country Y, tell business development to make it so, and it will happen. They can choose to change an incentive system from individual to group rewards, and HR will do it. However, you can't just decide to have more innovation. You can say it, order it, shout it really loudly, but that doesn't mean products will magically materialize. Innovation is a subtle process that involves many aspects of the organization, some of them tangible but many of them much more tacit and informal. And once those start to ossify, there's no pill that will cure that.

Framing something as a threat or an opportunity dramatically alters what we choose

So far, I have discussed how the mental models of our business and its environment are shaped by prior success and how they significantly influence people's decisions in terms of what course of action to pursue. Recall the research by Professors Allen Amason and Ann Mooney, discussed earlier in this chapter, which showed that CEOs from high-performance firms were inclined to interpret changes in their business environment as a threat, where CEOs of poorly performing companies tended to interpret changes as a positive thing? It reminded me of a famous experiment by Nobel Prize-winner Daniel Kahneman and Amos Tversky, which went as follows:

Imagine that the US is preparing for an outbreak of an unusual Asian disease, which is expected to kill 600 people. Two alternative programs to combat the disease have been proposed.

Assume that the exact scientific estimates of the consequences of the programs are as follows:

If program A is adopted, 200 will be saved.

If program B is adopted, there is a one-third probability that 600 people will be saved and a two-thirds probability that no people will be saved.

Which one of the two programs would you prefer?

Kahneman and Tversky found that a substantial majority of people would choose program A.

Then they gave another group of people the assignment but with the following description of the (same) options:

If program A is adopted, 400 people will die.

If program B is adopted, there is a one-third probability that nobody will die and a two-thirds probability that 600 people will die.

They found that, in this case, a clear majority of respondents favored program B! But the programs are exactly the same in both cases …!? How come people's preferences flip although they are confronted with the same set of choices (albeit described slightly differently)?

It is due to what we call "framing effects", and they greatly affect people's preferences and decisions. For instance, in the first case, program A is described in terms of the certainty of surviving (which people like), but in the second case it is described in terms of the certainty of dying (which people don't like at all!). Therefore, people choose A when confronted with the first program description, while in the second case they favor B, although the programs are the same in both situations.

We also see this influence in strategic decision-making, for instance in terms of whether particular environmental developments are "framed" as opportunities (which we like) or threats (which we don't like). A few years back, Clark Gilbert – at the time a professor at the Harvard Business School – analyzed American newspapers' responses to the rise of online media in the mid-1990s.

He found that those newspapers that, in their internal communications and deliberations, described online media as an opportunity (e.g., "a new avenue for attracting advertising revenue") coped quite well. In contrast, those newspapers that framed the exact same technological developments as a threat (e.g., "it will eat into our advertising market share") didn't cope well at all. In light of the threat, they reduced investments in experimentation, adopted a more authoritarian organization and management style, and focused more narrowly on their existing resources and activities. As a result, they basically ended up copying their physical newspaper onto the web; and that didn't work at all. Many of them didn't survive.

And this effect is omnipresent. How you frame decision-situations to someone (e.g., your boss) is going to influence substantially what option he is going to favor. How the people who work for you frame a situation while presenting to you is also going to determine what you will choose. And I guess that may be an opportunity (or a threat …) in and of itself.

In a downturn, manage your revenues, not your costs

All the subprocesses described in this chapter so far contribute to the success trap: the process of gradually getting stuck in what brought you success in the past, but which is currently causing you trouble. Hence, we know quite a bit, from research in organization science, about how firms end up in such a trap. Unfortunately, we know fairly little – hardly anything at all, to be honest – about what firms can actually do to get out of such a trap.

Since this, obviously and unfortunately, can be quite a relevant question for some (i.e., if you're in trouble), let me speculate a bit about what firms can attempt and do, once they have ended up in a crisis.

So, here's a hypothesis. In prosperous times, companies often fall victim to not being able to resist the many opportunities for growth that present themselves to them. In isolation, many initiatives with respect to new products, new markets, or new customers look good but when pursued in combination they have a negative effect and hamper growth. Wealthy firms find all these options difficult to resist precisely because in isolation they look so good. They have the funds to spare and therefore they are inclined to do too much of a good thing.

Andrew Grove, former CEO of Intel, understood this well. Intel's best-selling product – microprocessors – had endowed them with much cash to spare. However, he resisted the temptation to spend it on other initiatives and entering adjacent businesses, telling his people, "This is all a distraction; focus on job 1 [microprocessors]". It made them one of the most successful companies ever.

However, companies in distress – such as in a downturn – often do the reverse. In academic research, we call this the "threat-rigidity" effect. They focus on their core business, shedding all other things, doing more of what they did before, and which they consider their strongest points, while trying to reduce their cost base to weather the storm.

By itself, minimizing one's cost base is never a bad idea (also in prosperous times!) but these companies forget one thing: you have to manage not only your costs but also your revenues. And, what's more, the composition of a revenue base in lean times will have to look different from its composition when times are good. Where in happy times firms are often seduced to spread out too much, while they would be better off focusing on job 1, in meager times firms are often inclined to focus too much, when diversifying one's revenue base makes more sense.

So why does spreading one's revenue base in meager times make more sense? It is, among other reasons, because no job will be big enough to sustain the whole firm. What keeps firms afloat is accessing a variety of smaller pockets of revenues. Hence, rather than focus on job 1, hoping it will be enough to sustain the firm, the company's effort should be aimed at identifying and creating additional sources of revenue. In the downturn, none of these additional sources will be big enough by itself. Moreover, many of these sources would not be attractive in prosperous times, because the firm would not be able to make them grow. However, this is not a time of growth, but of survival.

A diversified revenue base will also reduce dependency and, with it, risk. In a downturn, the probability of individual sources drying up is large, so a firm can't afford to be focused on just one or a few of them.

But will searching for additional sources of revenue not be costly? If will not be costless but, by definition, it should not be expensive. Paradoxically, firms should not be focused on winning any big accounts, major new products or customers; they should aim for many smaller ones. They are relatively cheap to access and often the firm will already have knowledge about them; they may have shunned them in the past, considering them too small to advance at the time.

Concurrently, this strategy of exploring multiple smaller pockets of revenue will equip firms well for the economic dawn which will inevitably come. Their diverse revenue base has laid the foundation for new sources of growth. The firm will be able to quickly benefit from the upheaval in the economy. Many of the smaller pockets of revenue will stay small – and the firm would do well to shed quite a few of them – but the newly formed strategic landscape will be more conducive to different sources of revenue than before. Although you can't tell beforehand which ones it will be, some of the small pockets of revenue will be the new stars in the firm's firmament.

In a crisis, innovate

If you didn't buy that one, let me try another hypothesis (or, admittedly, a bit of the same wine in a different bottle): recently, an executive – an ex-student – told me about his company. The company had a handful of similar competitors (it is a local business) and they were all losing money in the challenging economic climate. Now one competitor – the worst-performing of the lot – had started to accept assignments for a fee below its cost price, just enough to cover its variable costs and at least earn back a tiny bit of its fixed costs. My ex-student asked me, "What can we do?"

The answer isn't easy. But it is of course a typical situation to be in. It happens in most industries in trouble; some bloody competitor – often the lousiest one of all – starts to sell below cost price, out of pure desperation. Actually, my ex-student's company responded in a way that is just as typical: they said, "But their product is inferior to ours; we deliver quality, and customers will always want to pay for that" (and stuck to their comparatively high price). But customers didn't. And they seldom do. Even if there is a minor quality difference – and it's usually just minor, at least in the eyes of the customer – if the price difference is large enough, you will lose a lot of clients; more than you can afford.

So what can you do? What else can you do but lower your prices too, tighten your belt, hold your breath, and hope the crisis blows over before you bankrupt yourself? Because that's what companies usually do.

I'd say the phenomenon is common, so the solution can't be.

It reminded me of the British newspaper business some years ago, which I briefly alluded to before. All quality newspapers were in trouble; newspapers had started to move online big time; free newspapers such as the *Metro* had flooded the market and, on top of that, the general trend was that people simply read less. The four main players in London – *The Guardian*, *The Times*, the *Daily Telegraph* and *The Independent* – were all in decline but *The Independent* was the one widely expected to fall first. The others had deep pockets due to rich owners and, thanks to a price war several years earlier, which had hit *The Independent* hardest, it was basically broke.

Now, *The Independent* could have done what most companies in such a situation do: moan about it, cut some more costs, and attempt to prolong an inevitable death. But it didn't. It took a plunge. It launched a small-sized version of its newspaper; the denounced "tabloid" format. All the newspapers had been talking about it for a long time, but everyone had dismissed it as too risky (customers won't like it), phoney, or plain cheap. But *The Independent* launched it, and it worked (customers loved it). They survived.

Was it a coincidence that out of the four main players it was *The Independent* that launched the thing? Of course not. It was *The Independent* that basically had nothing to lose; it would have been the first one to go under had the industry continued as it had been. But it chose to not just prolong its demise: it took a plunge, and recovered.

The same happened to Southwest Airlines. In its early days, when it was in deep trouble, it had to sell one of its four planes. Yet, it didn't try to just save some more costs and continue with 75 percent of its operations, prolonging an inevitable decline; it took a plunge. It said, "We're going to run 100 percent of our operations but with just three planes!" and, in the process, invented the widely successful low-cost airline model, having scrapped all frills and complications, combined with the emergence of a must-succeed culture.

❝ when you're down: innovate. Don't just wait for the inevitable to happen ❞

So, when you're down: innovate. Don't just wait for the inevitable to happen, prolonging your decline out of some false hope that you'll weather the storm. Storms kill; get out of it while you can.

Is your company brave enough to survive?

To be honest, in spite of my well-intended (and perhaps slightly desperate) speculations on the previous pages, my real answer, as a professor of strategic management, to the question, "What can our company do to survive the downturn?" should have been "I'm sorry, but not a lot".

❝ The market is Darwinian: the strongest ones survive. ❞

The market is Darwinian: the strongest ones survive. And an economic downturn is like winter in Alaska; many animals can live a happy life in Alaska all through spring, summer, and fall, but when winter comes, it's not a great place to be. It's a much tougher environment – and only the fittest survive.

If you're not very strong, if you haven't accumulated much body fat or haven't developed the ability to hibernate, I am afraid it is going to be tough for you, too. "But what can I do to become stronger? Get thicker skin? It's getting a bit cold here!" you might cry. Well, I am sorry (again), but winter in Alaska is not a great time to try and become stronger. It is just too late for that. But I do think there are a few survival techniques to be learned from looking at firms' downturn survival strategies, although they are not for the faint-hearted.

First, we see quite a lot of firms display what I earlier referred to as "threat-rigidity effects". When under threat, facing a shortfall in performance, firms are inclined to more narrowly and firmly focus on the one thing they do well (e.g., their core product or service), stop doing other things, and become more hierarchical and top-down in terms of management control. Unfortunately, this often makes things worse, or at least prevents you from coming up with any solutions.

What firms are better off doing is opening up: exploring new sources of potential revenue and experimenting with bottom-up processes to generate ideas and innovations. Let me give you an example. I am in touch with a company, in London, that provides custom-made software for all sorts of logistics systems, which they offer in combination with personnel training. Unfortunately, the vast majority of their customers are automotive companies, like General Motors and Ford ... clearly not a great position to be in right now. This recession has definitely been winter in Alaska for them, and at first they went through the usual cost-cutting and rounds of lay-offs.

After a while, though, the CEO decided to try something a bit different. He initiated some processes for all employees to start generating ideas for potential new sources of revenue, in which they enthusiastically participated (it was not like they had anything better to do ...). Most ideas were rubbish; some ideas were so-so, but a few ideas were really good! One of these ideas has now brought them a substantial new source of revenue.

One team had noticed that there was always one business unit doing well among their automotive customers; the unit providing spare parts. That's understandable; in a downturn, when people stop buying cars, more people need to have their cars repaired. And this greatly helps the spare parts units. So, this team decided to propose an inventory control product specifically aimed at the spare parts units of automotive companies. And it worked.

This is the opposite of the usual "threat-rigidity effects" – rather than focusing and becoming more narrow and top-down, this company opened up, organized bottom-up processes and tried something new. This is a brave thing to do, when winter blizzards are turning your ears frosty, because it feels like spending money rather than saving it. But finding the "spare parts division" among your customers might just see you through a downturn.

3

The urge to conquer

How big is your yam? (not that it matters)

Why are so many executives so preoccupied with the size of their company? As if bigger is always better. It especially annoys me when it is used as an excuse for acquisitions. "This take-over will immediately make us the largest company in the industry". So? What is your point?

I am sure being the biggest can have certain advantages, but that doesn't mean that bigger (let alone being the "biggest") is always automatically better. If you can explain to me why more scale is better, OK, but until then, I remain skeptical.

Of course company size is often associated with (financial) success. For example, the firms that always feature on "the most admired companies" lists are usually behemoths such as Toyota, Dell, Intel, Wal-Mart, and Pfizer. Several of them became big through acquisitions.

And I am sure a company worth $10 billion attracts quite a bit more attention (for instance in the business press) and admiration than any of the 10 companies that they acquired that were worth a mere $1 billion. But that doesn't mean that our $10 billion behemoth generates more profits than the 10 smaller ones would have made together. It wouldn't have been as eye-catching to have 10 small ones instead of one biggie, but it just might have made more sense (and money). Importantly, managers who opt for a strategy of increasing size reverse cause and effect; although success will likely make you bigger, striving for size is not necessarily going to make a company more successful.

This reminds me of the Aboriginals on the Micronesian island of Ponapae. What in their society contributed to a man's prestige was owning a very large yam. This cultural trait had come into existence because it represented an indication of a person's skill as a farmer. However, gradually people's efforts to obtain or grow one big yam started to be detrimental for their welfare, in the sense that it distracted effort and attention away from all other activities, causing malnourishment and hunger. People were putting all their resources, time, and effort into growing one giant yam, while their fields were left unattended, their huts crumbled around them, and their children cried of hunger.

Similarly, striving for size itself may be counter-productive for companies. It is quite possible that focusing all one's resources and efforts on becoming bigger (for the sake of being big) might actually decrease a firm's chances of becoming successful. Gaining size may result from firm success, but pursuing size, rather than success itself, may be quite detrimental.

66 striving for size itself may be counter-productive for companies 99

In Chapter 2 I showed why so often companies seem to grow fast and appear successful while some years later they are in dire straits. Using some clear concepts and examples I will now explain where the urge to grow fast comes from. I will also explain why it doesn't work. Specific attention is paid to the phenomenon of acquisitions and to the role of individual CEOs and their ambitions. I introduce the reader to Heineken (the company; not the beverage), provide some chilling facts about the success rate of acquisitions and, to lighten the mood, even share a joke (albeit not a very good one).

Deal-eager executives – tribal instincts

In this chapter, you will see quite a few references to studies in cultural and biological anthropology. That is because CEOs are human too (yes, really) and leading a firm often seems to unleash some primeval instincts. Moreover, an organization is, of course, at the end of the day, just a bunch of people. And bunches of people – whether a tribe, a company, or a mob – operate in particular, and often quite similar, ways.

❝ bunches of people – whether a tribe, a company, or a mob – operate in particular, and often quite ⸱ similar, ways ❞

You will see that, in this chapter, I also pay quite a bit of attention to acquisitions. This is because acquisitions especially seem to exemplify (and amplify) top managers' urge to rule and conquer. And that doesn't always bode well … Because where many top managers seem to be overjoyed by size, they are often outright gung-ho on acquisitions. These things really push the adrenaline pumps. Take Ahold's "fallen-from-grace" ex-CEO (now corporate convict) Cees van der Hoeven. Ahold actually started out with quite a careful approach to doing takeover deals, but over the years found itself completely out of control, like Imelda Marcos in a shoe shop.

My guess is there are two causes of deal-eager executives. It is the type of person who becomes CEO and it is the type of person we make them. Let me now discuss the first with you, and later in the chapter turn my attention to the second part.

An interesting line of research in social anthropology analyzed what type of person is more likely to rise through the ranks to become the head of a tribe. Often, this would be the most fierce, ambitious, and aggressive warrior, who would be willing to take on all his opponents in the quest for leadership.

Yet, interestingly, although characteristics such as fierceness and ambition would be helpful in becoming tribe leader, these characteristics were not necessarily positive for the future of the settlement, since these type of leaders were prone to take the tribe to war. This would ultimately take its toll on the size, strength, and survival chances of the tribe. Thus, the same characteristics that would make people more likely to become the head were likely to get the tribe into trouble.

CEOs might not be all that different. Those people who are ambitious, risk-seeking, and aggressive enough to be able to rise to the ultimate spot of CEO just might be the same people who, once they're there, take their firm on a conquest.

Acquisitions offer the thrill of the chase. You select a target, mobilize resources and lead the attack. Sometimes there are others eyeing your prey, but skillful maneuvering and a fierce battle will make you come out victorious again. And another victory means pictures in the newspapers, popping champagne, and a larger tribe to rule and command.

CEOs, marriage, mergers, geriatric millionaires, and blushing brides

Actually, I find it quite surprising how acquisitions, so openly, can get entangled with the personal aspirations and career progress of the companies' executives. For example, it is often thinly veiled that the single biggest hurdle to a particular merger, determining whether the deal will go through or not, is the question, "Who will be in charge afterwards?" The current CEO of company 1 or the CEO of company 2? The proposed merger between Dutch banks ING and ABN-Amro (before the financial crisis), for instance, was rumored to have fallen through because executives could not agree on who would take the helm. But are these really good, strategic, and legitimate reasons to pursue (or abolish) a deal? If you didn't notice, that was a rhetorical question ...

Similarly, in 1999, the merger of Viacom and CBS hinged on whether CEOs Sumner Redstone and Mel Karmazin could figure out how to distribute responsibilities and power. Eventually, the $40 billion mega-merger – at the time, the biggest media deal ever – seemed to be more of a declaration of love between the two than a move inspired by a clear strategic rationale.

For example, the LA Times referred to "secret meetings" between the two during which Redstone "grew to see the magic of the marriage Karmazin was proposing", while the New York Times quoted Redstone saying of Karmazin, "He is a master salesman, and he began to turn me on", also referring to "a marriage that was consummated after a two-year flirtation and a brief but painstakingly intense two-week prenuptial discussion. 'Mel seduced me', Redstone dreamily told reporters and investors after the merger was announced, sounding for all the world like a blushing bride."

Yet, the marriage came to an abrupt end in 2004, when Karmazin left acrimoniously. What turned out to be the case: Karmazin had negotiated, when the two were joined in holy matrimony in 1999, that if old Sumner (aged 81) happened to die during Karmazin's employment contract with Viacom, he would take the mantle. Yet, old Sumner didn't die ... and Karmazin was left waiting for his inheritance longer than he had anticipated. CBS and Viacom split in 2005.

To me, these kinds of negotiations suggest that the logic behind a deal may have more to do with advancing the careers of the people in charge, rather than advancing the value of the combined companies. If you're an investor or board member, I would conjecture that some suspicion may be warranted.

When acquisitions take over

We have seen many firms go on acquisitions sprees, inspired by their ambitious new CEO (who did not take long to go out in a blaze without much glory). The aggressiveness, boldness, and risk-taking behavior of the person at the helm had brought him to that position, but it sometimes does not translate well into a sensible corporate strategy. It outs itself in too many acquisitions, but also in paying too much for them.

Firms are expected to base the price and hence the premium they are willing to pay for a transaction on their calculations of how much synergy the deal would be able to generate. Although long-term value creation is always difficult to quantify with any certainty, firms usually do the best they can and then determine the target's maximum price.

However, once executives have their mind firmly set on acquiring a particular target but are outbid by a rival, this may be difficult to swallow. Often, it seems to awaken the warrior in them; they go back to their people and instruct them to "find me another 100 million or so in synergies" in the target's books, which enables them to up the bid. For instance, we saw indications of this when Mittal was bidding for Arcelor, and it is hardly unusual.

Clearly, this is a dangerous phase in a bidding process. Copious research, for instance on "escalation of commitment" (which I discussed in Chapter 2) in M&A deals has indicated that overexcited executives have a tendency not to walk away from a deal when they should, mysteriously uncovering extra value in a transaction when a firm's rivals are starting to outbid them. But I guess this bit is only human. It is the part which comes next that always gets me. The company that ultimately "wins" the bidding war is declared the winner – in newspapers, business magazines, etc. They pop the champagne and celebrate, while the loser pouts and has a crisis meeting.

But are we sure that you are the "winner" when you just paid 300 million for a company you originally calculated was worth half of that? And are you sure you really are the loser when you just made your competitor pay 150 million more than the darn thing is worth? Somehow, I am not so sure, no matter what the newspapers say.

"I STILL HAVE ONE MORE TAKE-OVER IN ME BEFORE I ENROLL IN AN ANGER MANAGEMENT PROGRAMME."

"Time compression diseconomies" – too much, too fast

The race to become big always reminds me of the cello lessons I had as a young boy. Let me explain: I started playing the cello when I was nine. And ever since, I have worried about time compression diseconomies. Yes, really. At the time, I didn't know they were called time compression diseconomies, but I did worry about them.

I used to have cello lessons on Saturday morning. I would play a certain piece in front of my teacher and then she would give me a new piece to practice for the next week.

Some weeks, I practiced for half an hour on Sunday, then half an hour on Monday, the same on Tuesday, etc., so by my next lesson, I would have practiced for a total of three hours (6 days; half an hour each). And I would usually be able to play the piece in front of my teacher reasonably well.

Some weeks, however, I did not practice on Sunday because I was out playing football. On Monday, I was at Boy Scouts, on Tuesday playing at a friend's house, on Wednesday I forgot about it altogether, and so on. By the time it was Friday, I would realize, "Oops, it's my cello lesson tomorrow, and I haven't practiced at all yet!"

What then I would usually do is think, "I will just practice for three hours in a row now; that's the same amount of time as half an hour each day for six days, and I am sure I will be fine." But I never was. It never worked. The noises coming out of my cello would be outright terrifying, reducing innocent passers-by to tears, with my teacher's ears (and mine) hurting for hours after she'd hastily sent me away.

And I wondered, as a nine-year-old, how is that possible? Three hours is three hours, right? Why does this not work: three hours on Friday instead of half an hour each day for six days in a row?

Of course, as adults, we realize that our brain needs rest in between practice sessions. It needs to recuperate before you can put new information and skills into it, and periods of inactivity are just as important as the practice itself. Practice sessions are much less effective if you don't have slow periods in between them.

Yet, nowadays, examining corporate strategy, I see many firms who have set themselves ambitious growth targets fall into the same trap. In order to catch up with competitors, for instance, they enter new markets at double the speed, undertake twice as many acquisitions, or hire double the number of employees. But, unfortunately, it doesn't work that way. Just like me practicing the cello, organizations need rest and time in between growth spurts to recuperate and digest the effort. Trying twice as hard does not mean you'll gain twice the benefits. There are limits to how fast you can grow, without starting to suffer from it.

> **❝ organizations need rest and time in between growth spurts to recuperate and digest the effort ❞**

We call this "time compression diseconomies" – a term coined by Professors Dierickx and Cool from INSEAD. When you, as an organization, try to compress lots of effort and growth into a short period, it will not be as effective as when you spread it out over a longer period of time (which is why we call them "diseconomies").

A large research project I undertook examining the growth strategies of 25 multinational companies showed exactly this: growing at a moderate yet steady pace increased profitability much more than did short outbursts of rapid expansion. And, unlike the effect of my youthful cello efforts on my teacher's auditive organs, these firms' performance really was music to their shareholders' ears.

Seeds and fertilizer – how to build a firm

American visitor: "How come you got such a gorgeous lawn?"

Lord: "Well, the quality of the soil is, I dare say, of the utmost importance".

American visitor: "No problem."

Lord: "Furthermore, one does need the finest quality seed and fertilizers."

American visitor: "Big deal."

Lord: "Of course, daily watering and weekly mowing are jolly important."

American visitor: "No sweat, just leave it to me!"

Lord: "That's it."

American visitor: "No kidding?! That's it?!"

Lord: "Oh, absolutely. There is nothing to it, old boy, just keep it up for five centuries."

The joke above – although admittedly not a very good one – makes a good point for the growth and management of organizations. What many firms, trying to grow fast or add scores of acquisitions, often fail to realize is that companies work in much the same way as a lawn. You can acquire all the individual elements – buy the machinery, lease the building, hire the people, acquire the assets, and so forth – pretty quickly and relatively easily, and put them together. But this does not mean that you will have a working organization.

An effective firm requires that the various elements of its organization – both the "hard" factors (such as its structure, incentive system, etc.) and the "soft" elements (such as the culture of the place, informal communication patterns, etc.) – are fine-tuned, interact with, and reinforce one another. Building such an organization implies more than just "owning the parts"; it takes continued dedication, hard work, and, most of all, it simply takes time.

This also has important implications for how you can create a competitive advantage. Often, we think of competitive advantage as something a firm has: a brand name, a set of patents, a unique location, and so forth. Things that, for competitors, are difficult to replicate so that it can give a firm a sustained advantage over them. However, what the anecdote above points out is that the organization itself can become a source of sustainable competitive advantage.

For example if, over the years, you have painstakingly built up a well-working organization in different parts of the world, active in different businesses, this can be very difficult for others to replicate. Competitors may be able to acquire all the pieces – subsidiaries and businesses in different parts of the world – and hence on paper look much the same, but in reality the organization will not work in the same way; they are loose pieces put together. This makes it all but impossible for rivals to catch up, even with a giant war chest and impressive acquisitions spree. Consequently, even without a particularly valuable patent, brand name, unique location, or value proposition in the market, you can build up a sustainable competitive advantage – but you have to be patient.

"I've won ... I've won!"

A striking example of several of the concepts discussed so far in this chapter concerns a company I first started studying when it was still on its way up (towards the sun ...): Ahold, and its larger-than-life CEO Cees van der Hoeven.

I first spoke to a member of its top management team in 1994, when I had started the research for my PhD thesis on international growth and acquisitions. I remember that he agreed to talk to me but only on a confidential basis because, as he declared, I was right that they did have an international presence but they were keen to not advertise that, because they cherished their image and reputation as an authentic, purely Dutch retailer. A bare five years later, when I finished my thesis work, they already got two-thirds of their revenue from the US alone, and had grown into a true multinational, being the third largest supermarket company in the world, trailing behind only Wal-Mart and Carrefour. Their international growth – mainly through acquisitions – had been truly massive and, to many, impressive.

It coincided with the reign of Cees van der Hoeven. Van der Hoeven, who grew up as a manager in Shell, had previously been the company's CFO. Yet, his lifelong ambition had always been to be a listed company's CEO and, when he finally made it to the top job, he famously shouted jubilantly in the company's corridors, "I've won … I've won!"

Ahold actually already had quite a significant presence in the US from the 1970s and 1980s, when they had acquired companies like BI-Lo, Giant Food stores, First National, and Tops supermarkets, after having examined at least a dozen other take-over candidates, conducting lengthy due diligence and a number of visits by all members of Ahold's management, including some posing as secret shoppers.

In 1993, when Cees van der Hoeven took the top job, he wanted to double Ahold's revenues and profit in five years, while growing earnings per share of at least 10 percent per year. In the same year, Ahold received the Investor Relations Award in the Netherlands, while Ahold entered Eastern Europe, Portugal, and Singapore. After several years of solid double-digit growth, winning the Dutch Invester Relations Award back-to-back, Van der Hoeven independently announced that the profit growth expectations for the next five years were to be increased to 15 percent. In 1996, in just a few months, Ahold consecutively entered five new markets: Thailand, Malaysia, Spain, China, and Brazil.

However, the acquisition targets appear to not have been examined with the same scrutiny as in the past, and murmurs started that they were also poorly integrated. In 1997, one of the longest-serving top management-team members took early retirement, and during his farewell speech spoke directly to Van der Hoeven: "Cees, you shouldn't try to become the biggest, but the best; then you'll automatically become the biggest." However, in 1997 Ahold commited to a profit increase of between 30 and 45 percent and again won the Dutch Investor Relations award. In 1998, Van der Hoeven announced that in the coming five years, Ahold will again double in size.

During the management team's traditional Monday afternoon lunch – a weekly event dubbed the "acquisition lunch" – the team approved a significant number of take-overs on four different continents. One of them, the American company

Pathmark, Ahold had earlier dismissed as of insufficient quality, because their explicit criteria had always been to only acquire companies that were top players in terms of their profitability. When questioned, Van der Hoeven stated that an acquisition target does not need to be a top player in terms of profitability, but rather in terms of "profit potential".

Yet, after mounting problems in various subsidiaries, in 1999, an internal audit concluded that between 30 to 40 percent of the visited subsidiaries did not have adequate control. While the board expressed their concerns, van der Hoeven won the Dutch CEO of the Year award. In the subsequent year, 2000, competitor Delhaize acquired Hannaford Brothers, which Ahold had explicitly earmarked as an ideal acquisition target. Next, Carrefour managed to acquire the Promodes chain. Analysts began to express doubts about whether the company could fulfill van der Hoeven's promise of 15 percent annual growth. British chain Tesco was suggested as a potential target, but the secret negotiations between Ahold and Tesco had already ended unsuccessfully.

Van der Hoeven and his team responded in true Ahold style, and acquired 50 percent of the large Scandinavian company ICA. It also acquired American Internet-grocer Peapod and several business-to-business firms, including US Foodservice (of which Van der Hoeven declared "six months ago, US Foodservice was not even on our list of candidates"), as well as the supermarket chain Bruno's, which had earlier filed for Chapter 11 bankruptcy. Ahold again won the Dutch Investor Relations Award and the Dutch Reputation Award of 2001. The thirteen acquisitions in 2000 had added 3,600 shops to Ahold's original 4,500, spreading it over 24 countries, resulting in a strategy which they stated was "multi-format, multi-local, multi-channel".

Yet, while van der Hoeven continued to affirm that they needed "strong targets" and "outrageous goals" and Ahold was named US Retailer of the Year, in early 2002 serious conflicts began to arise in the Czech Republic, the Netherlands, and in Scandinavia, while the tensions in Portugal continued to spiral out of control.

On July 4th, 2002, Ahold issued its first profits warning, swiftly followed by a second one on November 19th, then immediately announced its seventh take-over in the US foodservice market. An inquiry by the firm's internal accountants revealed that $30–35 million were used as illicit commission in Argentina. Regardless of its growing problems, Ahold won the Dutch Reputation Award in 2002, beating other top candidates such as Heineken and Ikea.

February 2003 brought about Ahold's largest scandal: financial fraud at US Foodservice, which eventually accrued to $880 million claimed in unrealized profits. In March 2003, the board fired van der Hoeven. Several years and one court trial later, he received a suspended jail sentence for his role in the financial malversation.

The story of Ahold is a typical one. In hindsight, we all think how could that happen? This house was bound to collapse! But at the time we all bought into it, both their groceries and their shares. That's because it is not a one-man story; surely van der Hoeven was an overly deal-eager guy with an eerie resemblance to Icarus, but it is also a story about time compression diseconomies, an over-reliance on numbers, a strategy adapted to a firm's actions (rather than the other way around), and one very big yam. And this concerns a whole management team, boards, banks, shareholders, analysts, award committees, the business press, and business schools (who audaciously write management cases and give honorary degrees for stories that are too good to be true). It is a whole system. And the system may at some point push people towards the sun, to subsequently watch their fall, shaking their heads in disbelief.

Most acquisitions fail – really!

Of course, acquisitions also played a huge role in the Ahold story. The processes that lead firms to take on too many acquisitions, too fast, are much the same processes that lead them to pay too much for their takeovers. The former lead to poor integration and little value creation; the latter lead to very high acquisitions premiums. Acquisition premiums – the amount of money the acquiring firm pays on top of what the target is currently worth – are often quite astronomical; 70–80 percent above the company's current worth is not unusual (so perhaps "astrological" would have been a more accurate description ...). A very high price, in combination with little value creation, is a lethal mix.

And I have little doubt that this forms the main reason why the track record of acquisitions, in terms of their success rate (to create extra value), is truly abysmal. So let me show you the stats on M&A again: you may have seen them before, but since I am sure you may (still) not believe them, here they are once more.

Seventy to eighty percent of acquisitions fail, in terms of creating stock-market value. Two overview studies in the prestigious *Strategic Management Journal* showed that, on average, share prices of acquiring companies fall between 0.34 percent and 1 percent in the ten days following the announcement of an acquisition. And this is a result consistent over a period of 75 years of stock-market data!

"But that's only 10 days," you might say. "These acquisitions might still create value in the long run, right?" Nope; wrong. Research in the *Journal of Finance* concluded that acquiring firms experience a wealth loss of 10 percent over the five years after merger completion.

"Perhaps the stock market initially is too pessimistic?" Actually, quite the opposite: a study on 131 big deals (over $500 million) indicated that in 59 percent of cases, market-adjusted return went down on announcement. Hence, the stock market was positive about 41 percent of deals. Not an awful lot, but it could have been worse. Or could it...?

After 12 months, 71 percent of all those deals had negative consequences! That is, of the 41 percent of cases where market value went up on announcement because the stock market was optimistic about their potential to create value, only 55 percent still had positive returns the year after! Thus, even the stock market had initially been way too optimistic. Even more deals ended up destroying value than they had first expected.

Yet, every time I show these statistics to a group of executives they frown and proclaim, "We know this, but it is not true for our company." Often followed by, "We analyzed all our deals and two-thirds were a success" (not sure why it is always two-thirds, but it always is). Yeah, right.

Almost invariably, it concerns a round of interviews or perhaps a questionnaire, sometimes supplemented by a few tables and figures of dubious descent, asking some people in the business whether they thought a particular deal was a success. Now, if these people say "no" to this (almost rhetorical) question, you can bet it was nothing short of a disaster.

Of all the deals conducted, this leaves two-thirds of "non-disasters", which is not the same as successes. Perhaps another third did not cause major problems as the integration went OK, but that does

not mean that the (usually very expensive) deal actually created value – at least beyond the take-over premium that was paid. You might have been better off not having done it at all, despite having avoided a disaster.

So, believe me, two-thirds of acquisitions fail – yes, really.

"Heerlijk, helder, Heineken"

Now, I realize it is about time that I said something nice about the practice of acquisitions. Since I have been known to sound slightly skeptical (yes, this is a good English euphemism) about the vehicle of corporate takeovers, people sometimes ask me which company's acquisition strategy I actually like. A painful silence (to this fair question) used to ensue. But no longer! Since I didn't want to create the erroneous impression that I think all acquisitions and acquirers are bad, I decided to look for one.

And I found "heerlijk, helder, Heineken". Which probably doesn't mean much to you, unless you're Dutch. It translates into something like "divine, clear, Heineken", and it happens to be the old marketing slogan of a product that I studied extensively during my student days. Having grown up (with regret), some time ago I also really dug into their past acquisition strategy, to see whether it made any sense. And I had to say "heerlijk, helder, Heineken" or, in English, "yes".

No, I am not getting a commission for rehashing their old marketing slogan: it just reminds me of the acquisition strategy they used under the reign of their illustrious former chairman Freddy Heineken (who unfortunately died a number of years ago).

This is what I like about it: many managers see acquisitions as a relatively and easy quick way to increase the size of their company, in comparison to the painstaking process of organic growth. Yet, they forget that owning a bunch of companies doesn't necessarily turn them into one organization. Successful companies often have a high level of co-ordination between the various activities and parts of their organization. This involves technology and systems but also intangible characteristics such as a shared culture and informal networks; just like the English lord's lawn I introduced earlier in this chapter. Research by Wenpin Tsai and Sumantra Ghoshal, published in the *Academy of Management Journal*, showed that these organizational abilities take time to grow and develop. Freddy Heineken realized this; he did quite a few acquisitions, but not too many, and carefully added and integrated them into his company. Moreover, he did not see them as a substitute for organic growth but, instead, as an enabler of it. He used to undertake acquisitions with the explicit aim of creating further opportunities for organic growth both for the acquired company (which benefited from Heineken's knowledge, purchasing power, and management capability) and for the Heineken brand (which benefited from added local distribution).

> ❝ Freddy used to say, "I don't want to be the biggest; I want to be the best." And, as a result, he was. ❞

Heineken's focus was always on profitability, rather than scale *per se*. This made him stubbornly resist loud calls (for instance, by analysts and investors, and some business school professors …) to merge with a major rival. Freddy used to say, "I don't want to be the biggest; I want to be the best." And, as a result, he was.

Toads and acquisitions – where does CEO "hubris" come from?

Most acquisitions don't create much value. The famed investor, Warren Buffett, once said that many corporate acquirers think of themselves as beautiful princesses, sure that their kisses can turn toads into handsome princes. The acquirers pay substantial premiums over market value, believing that they can release the imprisoned princes. But, as Buffett said, "We've observed many kisses but very few miracles."

Because, as discussed before, when a firm acquires another company, it usually pays a hefty premium. That is, the firm pays quite a bit more for the company's shares than the price it is trading at on the stock market before the takeover, just to be able to obtain a majority, and hence a controlling, stake.

According to academic research, this premium usually lies somewhere between a whopping 50 and 70 percent, dependent on the industry, the size of the firm, etc. The justification for paying such a significant premium is the idea that the acquiring firm will be able to get much more value out of the company than the seller does. As I've said before, the facts show that they're usually wrong, but firms still do it!

It gets interesting when you analyze who pays the biggest premiums. My former colleague at the London Business School, Mathew Hayward, now at the University of Colorado, together with his colleague Don Hambrick, performed a slightly mischievous analysis. They figured that CEOs who are full of themselves would pay higher premiums – because they suffer from "hubris" and are more likely to overestimate their own ability to turn around "failing" companies. Therefore, they counted the number of favorable articles that had appeared about them in the business press (such as *The Financial Times*, *Business Week*, etc.).

Subsequently, they computed whether CEOs who had received more media praise paid more for their acquisitions. The answer was: absolutely YES!! To be precise, each highly favorable article about a company's CEO would increase the premium paid by no less than 4.8 percent. For an acquisition of a billion dollars, this would equate to 48 million dollars ... And that is for every article!

And this really is $48 million down the drain, because Hayward and Hambrick also showed that CEOs with more favorable press were completely unable to create additional value out of those acquisitions. They had simply overestimated themselves.

It is tempting to blame these stupid, arrogant executives, and their silly companies and boards. However, what I find equally interesting is that this research also indicates where hubris comes from: it comes from us! We glorify top managers, print their pictures in newspapers and magazines, praise their decisiveness and vision, give them awards, and treat them like superstars. All they're guilty of – the poor bastards – is believing the BS we write about them.

4

Gods and villains

The heroes of our time

Continuing where the previous chapter left off, this chapter is specifically dedicated to the eye-catching phenomenon of CEOs. CEOs, to many people, are the heroes of our time. They are the topics of news stories, business-school cases, and biographies. They become celebrities, heroes, and superstars, prone to deification, sometimes attaining almost God-like status (such as GE's Jack Welch). We place them on the cover of magazines such as *Fortune* and *Business Week*, we give them awards, honorary doctorates, and multi-million salary packages, while they command dazzling fees for after-dinner speeches, at which they are drenched in the adoration of star-struck hopefuls, who quench their thirst for personal business success on the (expensive) words of the great leader.

Yet, just as easily, it seems, they can fall from grace and personify the failure of an entire conglomerate (such as Enron's Jeff Skilling).

This chapter discusses these processes, providing examples and evidence from research. It argues that "it is the type of people that become CEOs" but also shows evidence that it is the world which makes them that way. I will explain to you why the most successful CEOs, by definition, are incompetent, take you to an awards dinner in New York City, and present to you a little piece of statistical analysis that shows when CEOs are most likely to pass the baton. Finally, to discuss a vital, yet often overlooked role of a business leader, I provide the example of Stevie Spring, a CEO who jokingly calls herself a CST – a Chief Story-Teller.

Narcissus versus Humble Bloke – and the winner is ...?

Have you heard of Narcissus, the character in Greek mythology? Narcissus was an exceptionally beautiful young man. He was so beautiful (and full of himself) that he fell in love with his own reflection. He could not bring himself to stray from the well and did not even drink the water, fearing he'd disturb the water reflecting his image and would not see himself again. Our word "narcissistic" – to describe someone full of himself – is derived from him.

How would you recognize a narcissistic CEO (as certainly not all of them are exceptionally beautiful)? Seriously, think about it, what would you say are the signs of a CEO who is narcissistically full of himself?

Someone who always has his photograph displayed prominently in his firm's annual report? The CEO's prominence in the company's press releases? How often he uses first-person singular pronouns (such as I, me, mine, my, myself) giving interviews to the business press? Or his financial compensation relative to the second-highest paid executive in his firm?

Arijit Chatterjee and Donal Hambrick, of Pennsylvania State University, measured all of these things, among 111 CEOs, and used them to construct a measure of their narcissism. They selected their 111 CEOs from the computer hardware and software industries because prior writers on leadership had suggested that narcissism in a CEO might actually be a good thing in very dynamic, fast-changing industries, which these two are. They then examined a bunch of characteristics of a firm's strategy, to figure out what narcissistic CEOs do differently

❝ narcissistic CEOs favor bold actions that attract attention, resulting in big wins or big losses ❞

than their more humble counterparts (in between periods of staring at their own reflection, I guess).

And guess what, they found that the more narcissistic types changed their firm's strategy more often than the humble blokes. Moreover, they also tended to undertake a lot more – and a lot bigger – acquisitions. The performance of their corporations (perhaps partly as a consequence) fluctuated quite heavily, in comparison with the humble types.

But what about the *level* of their firms' performance: it may have fluctuated more but did the narcissistic guys on average achieve higher or lower performance? Neither. They didn't do better, and they didn't do worse (both in terms of return on assets and total stock-market performance).

Arijit and Don concluded "that narcissistic CEOs favor bold actions that attract attention, resulting in big wins or big losses, but that their firms' performance is generally no better or worse than firms with non-narcissistic CEOs".

However, I'd say they're worse; you're better off without them. It is not only money that matters; these types are plain annoying. If they don't bring in more dosh than their more pleasant counterparts, you're better off with humble bloke.

Are overconfident CEOs born or made?

But where does narcissism come from? One good context to assess this question is M&A: one firm buying the next.

But let me first remind you: most acquisitions fail. That's not even a point of debate or opinion anymore; the evidence from ample, solid academic research is quite overwhelming: about 70 percent of acquisitions destroy value, and this has been the case for many, many decades.

❝ But let me first remind you: most acquisitions fail. ❞

The question is what causes managers to undertake them in spite of their dismal track record? One prominent explanation, as discussed in previous chapters, is that the average CEO suffers from "hubris" or "overconfidence". They think they will be able to create more value through the acquired company than the silly people who are currently running the show, because they're much better and smarter than the sorry souls who are currently messing about in that block of bricks they call a firm.

Therefore they're willing to pay an acquisition premium. Yet, it's apparent that usually they are overestimating their abilities, because the average CEO/acquisition does not create any surplus value – quite the contrary. Fact is (assuming that managers are well-intended and do expect to create value through their acquisitions; though some people even disagree with this assumption), on the whole, one can only conclude that most of them are overconfident because in 70 percent of the cases they don't manage to pull it off.

But, to get back to the matter in hand, where does their overconfidence come from? Does the average CEO suffer from hubris because that's the type of person who makes it to the top? That's one possibility. The other one is that, over the course of their tenure, top managers often gradually become overconfident, rather than suffering from hubris from the get-go.

❝ overconfident CEOs are made and not born that way ❞

Professors Matthew Billett and Yiming Qian from the University of Iowa examined this exact issue, using a sample of 2,487 American CEOs undertaking a combined 3,795 deals over the period 1980–2002, and they found some very compelling evidence that overconfident CEOs are made and not born that way.

They initially uncovered four things.

1　They discovered that CEOs' first deals, on average, did *not* destroy value: their effect on a company's market value was pretty much zero.

2　Those CEOs who had experienced a negative stock-market

effect in response to their first acquisition usually lost their appetite for doing any more deals.

3　In contrast, those CEOs who – hurrah! – had experienced a positive stock-market response to their first takeover got the hots for deal-making; they were very likely to undertake even more acquisitions in the ensuing years.

4　Those subsequent deals, however – that is, takeovers by CEOs who had done some before – on average *did* destroy shareholder value! Hence, the consistent finding in academic research that acquisitions destroy value seems to be caused by CEOs' later deals only.

Matthew and Yiming concluded that first-time, successful deals make CEOs overconfident, which not only stimulates them to do even more deals, but also makes them inclined to pay even heftier takeover premiums for subsequent ones, which they are usually unable to recoup after the acquisition.

Finally, they also examined "insider trading": whether CEOs would purchase their own company's stock in the period preceding the acquisition (confident that it would increase in value as a result of the deal). Most CEOs did, whether they were first-time deal-makers or experienced acquirers. However, the effect for experienced acquirers (people who had done deals before) was twice as big as for the novices. Apparently, overconfident serial acquirers – who usually ended up destroying shareholder value – most of the time fell into their own hole; they bought the shares whose value they were about to destroy! Guess there's a hint of justice in this story after all ...

Hang the hero

There are ample examples of top managers who start to personify their company and its success, because we see them on TV and read about them in our newspapers and websites on a daily basis: Steve Jobs and Apple, Carlos Ghosn and Nissan and, of course, Jack Welch and GE.

❝ CEOs can become villains ❞

Similarly, CEOs can become villains. They start to personify the misery that their organization has brought us. We mock them, vilify them and, if we get the chance, put them in jail. Cees van der Hoeven – who got off with a suspended jail sentence – personified Ahold's fall from glory; Enron's Jeff Skilling is spending 24 years in a prison in Minnesota (of all places), while former media mogul Conrad Black caught some rays of sunshine through the bars of his cell in Florida.

But do we really believe that organizations consisting of 100,000 employees, located on various continents in all corners of the world, producing dozens of products in a multitude of industries and markets, are controlled by the lunch-time decisions of one man? Can one man be that omnipotent?

I guess these attributions are not restricted to business leaders. Tolstoy had a clear opinion on the aforementioned (admittedly rhetorical) question. In his great novel *War and Peace*, reflecting on the eventual defeat of Napoleon's forces in Russia after the battle of Borodino, he was skeptical of any attributions of omnipotence. He wrote:

"Many historians contend that the French failed at Borodino because Napoleon had a cold in the head, and that if it had not been for this cold … Russia would have been annihilated and the face of the world would have been changed."

"If it had depended on Napoleon's will whether to fight or not to fight the battle of Borodino, or had it depended on his will whether he gave this order or that, it is evident that a cold affecting the functioning of his will might have saved Russia, and consequently the valet who forgot to bring Napoleon his waterproof boots on the 24th would be the saviour of Russia."

"But for minds which cannot admit that Russia was fashioned by the will of one man … such reasoning will seem not merely unsound and preposterous but contrary to the whole nature of human reality. The question, 'what causes historic events?' will suggest another answer, namely, that the course of earthly happenings … depends on the combined volition of all who participate in those events, and that the influence of a Napoleon on the course of those events is purely superficial and imaginary."

I think we also overdo it a bit when we bestow our complete and unreserved adoration on the CEOs of successful corporations. But similarly, perhaps we also tend to overdo it a bit when we vilify the CEOs of companies that have failed?

Perhaps one extreme (and sad) example of the latter is Warren Anderson, the former CEO of Union Carbide, who was in charge of this behemoth of a company on December 3rd 1984, when one of its plants, in Bhopal in India, caused what is perhaps the most dreadful industrial accident in the history of mankind. A leak of poisonous gas killed thousands of people on the dreadful day itself, while tens of thousands of people perished in its aftermath.

The people from Bhopal viewed – and still view – Warren Anderson as the prime instigator of the evil that befell them. They still paint "Hang Anderson" on the city's walls and burn puppets in his imagery. Was Warren Anderson responsible? I am sure he was; he played his part being in charge of the company that owned 51 percent of the factory. The personal anger of the people of Bhopal is understandable, just as the adoration of Jack Welch *et al.* seems to satisfy some deep human inclination to create gods. But, in reality, both the success and the downfall of our organizations are, as Tolstoy put it, the result of "the combined volition of all who participate in those events". When we glorify the individual we might be exaggerating; when we vilify the fallen we might be overdoing it too.

❝ When we glorify the individual we might be exaggerating; when we vilify the fallen we might be overdoing it too. ❞

Celebrity CEOs and the burden of expectations

One great scientific study on celebrity CEOs examined the consequences of receiving awards. It focused on the former business magazine *Financial World*, which had an annual and widely publicized contest called CEO of the Year. Based on a survey of a large number of analysts and CEOs, they awarded medals to the top executives of a number of large American firms. A couple of thousand CEOs were eligible; they gave out a few hundred bronze medals, about a dozen silver medals, and one gold medal to the true God of Business. The medals were awarded during a lush and golf-anecdote-friendly dinner in New York City. The magazine has long gone bust (although, reportedly, throwing lush dinners till the bitter end) but its awards continue to echo a telling tale.

A few years ago, together with some colleagues, Professor James Wade from Georgetown University examined what happened to these award-winning CEOs and their companies following the receipt of the prestigious prize. They first analyzed whether the companies of the award-winners actually did any better than the awardless schmucks, and the answer was "nope". Professor Wade and his colleagues put it a bit more carefully, saying that "star CEOs have neither a positive nor a negative effect on the operating results of firms" but, of course, this basically means: nope.

They then analyzed whether the star CEOs made more money (for themselves) than the hapless schmucks, in the form of the size of compensation package they were given by their boards subsequent to being awarded the medal. And the answer was a profound "yes" – that is, with one caveat. Winning a medal increased a CEO's pay by about 10 percent but if the company displayed bad performance (as bad as a *negative* return on equity), the lauded CEO would actually make *less* money than his medal-craving counterparts. Apparently boards are suckers for stardom, in terms of compensating their prized CEOs, but when these captains severely underdeliver they will also punish them for it.

Yet, for CEO remuneration this negative effect was relatively weak; after all, there are not many companies around with negative ROE. The stock market, as usual, was more ruthless. Jim and his colleagues also examined how the stock market responded to the CEO receiving an award. Initially, the stock market (and, importantly, its share price graph) made a little jump of joy (of about a quarter of a percent). However, for the average firm, after a few days, the share price started decreasing, and it kept decreasing for months. After about eight months, the stock market rated the firms of award winners more than 8 percent lower than the unlauded CEOs' shops. Eight percent! For a billion-dollar company, this basically means that your CEO getting a medal knocks 80 million bucks off your firm's value! That's one mighty expensive medal.

How come the effects of receiving an accolade can be so negative? I guess it is all about expectations. Recall that the initial effects – both in terms of the CEO's remuneration and in terms of the stock-market response – were positive. But after a while they turned nasty; if the CEO couldn't meet the heightened expectations, the stock market especially responded with disappointment, and shareholders voted with their feet. And Jim's research shows that the average CEO could not live up to the expectations.

Awards may heighten a CEO's pay check and make the stock market buzz with anticipation, but they also heighten expectations; if these expectations are not met, the award will come back to haunt you. And I am sure that is not what they had in mind when the cameras flashed while they proudly accepted the prized medal at their black-tie Manhattan dinner.

Successful managers – incompetent for sure

One could doubt whether our celebrity CEOs really outperform their more anonymous counterparts; certainly there is no evidence to suggest that they do any better. Some would even go a step further, and boldly argue where no-one has argued before, namely that the highest-performing CEOs are also the dumbest of all ... Let me explain:

The world of business is risky. That's inevitable. We can analyze all we want, plan, debate, gather information and think it through

> **❝ The world of business is risky. That's inevitable. ❞**

till it gives us a migraine, but sometimes things just don't work out and nobody could have foreseen it.

So what makes for a good risk manager? Well, it is someone who carefully chooses the best odds. He will sometimes win, and sometimes lose. But, he will always make deliberate and careful trade-offs between his assessment of risk and return: the most expected return for the least risk. Sometimes good managers accept a low return when it is safe (like buying government bonds); sometimes they accept a lot more risk in return for a higher expected return (like investing in the stock market).

Bad managers are those people who just don't get it. They accept worse average returns for higher risks. Clearly that's dumb. But it is also where it gets tricky. Because if they accept very high risks, in spite of lower average returns, every once in a while one of these morons will actually hit the jackpot ...* That is, if we take the top one percent of top performers, they're likely to be those people who didn't get it at all ... but just got incredibly lucky!

The same is true – as Stanford's Professor Jim March asserted – for CEOs. The ones that are the eye-catching top performers are likely the ones who just don't get it. The dangerous thing is that they are also the ones with the absolute highest return in their business. Therefore we naïvely believe that they "do get it" and, in fact, are quite brilliant. Moreover, that's what they start to believe as well ("I win again; I must be brilliant!"). Yes, they got lucky once, they might get lucky twice, or three times (at which point we start to notice them) but eventually their luck will turn (Bernard Tapie, Jeff Skilling, Cees van der Hoeven, and Conrad Black come to mind).

---

* In statistical terms, good managers have a normal distribution around a relatively high average; bad managers have a lower average return but a distribution with "fat tails". Consequently, because of the long right-hand tail, the top performers stem from the "bad managers" distribution/pool.

The same is often true for fund managers, and other people who are trying to make money on the stock market. The top-performing funds are not necessarily the best ones when it comes to ability. For example, have you ever come across these competitions in which people receive a starting sum to "play the stock market" and after six months or so the person with the highest return wins a prize or even a job? Stupid scheme by design: the person with the highest return is by definition the one that really did not have a clue, because the only way to win such a contest is by making the most silly, illogical, and risky allocation of funds, and get lucky. Skillful, careful players will not lose their money, and likely get a decent return, but won't be the ones to come out on top.

And the issue is: some bloke will get lucky. Ninety-nine out of a hundred cases it will go wrong, but the ultimate winner is dumbo number one hundred. The contest by sheer design ends up picking a nitwit as the winner.

Hence, watch out for "top performers" in any business or situation which involves risk. The one coming out on top is likely to be a moron who just got lucky.

Executives: superhuman after all ...

Where the previous deliberation may be extreme, I do think it is true that we are usually not very good at explaining and attributing success – especially when it comes to ourselves.

It is a well-known aspect of our everyday behavior: when we perform well, we take the credit ourselves; when something goes wrong we blame something (or someone) else. This effect –

known as attribution bias – has been well-documented by social psychologists, but I guess we didn't really need their research; it is a common phenomenon in everyday life.

Professors John Wagner and Richard Gooding, at Michigan State University, examined whether managers suffer from the same bias. They rounded up 102 executives and subjected them to some lengthy experiments and statistical analysis – I won't bore you with the details because the answer was (surprise, surprise) "yes". When a company's performance is great, executives claim (and actually believe!) that it is due to their brilliant efforts; when, vice versa, their company's performance sucks, it's someone else's fault and they're really, really not to blame, honest. Yep, executives are just like humans.

Then, however, John and Richard did something rather interesting. They not only asked these executives to interpret the performance of their own companies (as explained above); they also asked them what they thought caused the performance of their peers/competitors.

As I said, when their own company was performing well they attributed it to their own efforts, while when they were performing

" NORMALLY I WANT RESULTS AND NOT EXCUSES
HIGGINS, BUT THESE ARE BRILLIANT... "

badly they blamed external circumstances. Yet, when assessing their colleagues' performance, the bias flipped! When other executives' firms performed well, the managers said "it's due to some external circumstances" while when their colleagues' firms were underperforming, they attributed it to these persons' errors! This behavior had not been documented before among humans. So I guess we can either conclude from this that managers are borderline human, or perhaps that they ae even more human than the rest of us ... Take your pick.

"Over the hill and far away, top managers are here to stay"

The gap between being a hero and villain is sometimes scarily small. And, for a CEO, it is easy to find yourself being thrown from left to right, but making your way back is a sheer impossibility. When your board finally boots you out due to the company's persistent poor performance, that might be it for you; your reputation is tarnished and you will find your boardroom employability has reached that of an alcoholic applying for a job at a liquor store. Firm performance is obviously a big influence on when top executives leave, even when the press release tries to paint a different picture. Top managers often pass the baton, and move on to "seek other challenges" simply because they are forced to do so by their boards.

Yet, *poor* performance appears not to be the only cause for premature departure. Academic research on American executives – by, among others, Professors Wagner, Pfeffer, and O'Reilly – has shown that top managers are not only leaving when the performance of their companies is rock bottom (undoubtedly with a good poke by their board if not a kick in the backside) but also when firm performance is relatively high. Wagner speculated that this happens because then they're hot stuff on the job market and able to find themselves a nice new green pasture.

Now, although this will hardly be anyone (else)'s idea of "fun", it so happened I had a database available on a couple of hundred

Dutch top managers and was curious about whether the same might be true for these guys (yes, all of them guys ...). And you know what, after a good chunk of statistical analysis on a rainy afternoon, it appeared that Dutch top managers also leave when their firm's performance is at a high. Yet, they're not walking at all when it's low?! Apparently, Dutch top managers don't easily get the sack even if their firms are underperforming.

Interestingly, though, these top managers not only left when their firm's performance was relatively high, but when it was also just starting to (rapidly) decline. With their image intact, and their successor in place, they left before the slide. I guess it is all about picking your moment; what better time to get out than when you're just "over the hill", and your house of cards may be about to come tumbling down.

Chief story-teller

The question remains, what do CEOs really do? Because, although their impact might sometimes be overrated (for better and for worse), they certainly have some influence. What is the role of a CEO?

Stevie Spring, CEO of Future plc (a UK magazine publisher), recently expressed it to me in the following way: "I am not really the Chief Executive; I am the Chief Story-Teller." What (on earth) did she mean by that?

Let's first think, what is an organization? Well, it is a group of people – sometimes a rather large group of people – (supposedly) working towards a common goal. This goal may simply be profit, but it certainly helps if we have a common idea of what we're trying to do in order to make a profit. Hence, it is about setting a clear strategic direction. A clear strategic direction is not a 40-page document outlining a firm's strategy – that's a drawer-filler. It is a concise set of choices that determines what we do and don't do. For example,

> ££ A clear strategic direction is a concise set of choices that determines what we do and don't do. ””

for Future it's something like "special interest, English-language magazines for young males, possibly with spill-overs online and in terms of events". Hence, they would for instance do a magazine on "guitar rock" but not on "music" (as that is not focused enough to be considered a special interest); they would do such a magazine in the US but not in German (then they might license it); they would cover motorcycle racing, or Xbox or wind-surfing, but not knitting (unless, without me realizing it, knitting has recently had a popularity surge in the community of 20-something males). Thus, it determines what you do, but it also determines what you don't do, because it doesn't fit your expertise and capabilities.

And Stevie Spring tells that story – over and over again – to a variety of constituents: to analysts and fund managers, board of directors, employees, customers, and even the occasional business-school professor.

Good CEOs have a story. Tony Cohen of Fremantle Media says they want television productions to which they own the rights, with spin-offs in other areas (e.g., online), which are replicable in different countries – simple and focused. Alistair Spalding of London's Sadler's Wells theater wants to be actively involved in producing a broad array of cutting-edge modern dance, aimed at a London audience. Frank Martin of Hornby wants to produce near-perfect scale models of model trains (and Scalextric race tracks) for collectors and hobbyists, which appeal to some feeling of nostalgia. Their stories are clear and simple; employees, investors, and customers alike can understand and believe in them.

Is being able to tell a convincing story enough for a good strategy? I don't think so. I remember a Goldman Sachs analyst writing about Enron in October 2001 (weeks before its bankruptcy), "Enron is still the best of the best. We recently spoke with most of its top management; our confidence level is high."

However, a convincing story certainly helps. When you have a lousy strategy, without much focus or logic to it, it is hard to come up with a coherent and convincing story. And it's a good story that makes people want to invest in you, that carries the day when you need your board's support (e.g., when making tough choices on what to divest or invest in), and that helps your employees see their tasks and decisions in light of the company's overall direction. It's the strength of the story that makes the CEO.

Managers and leaders: are they different?

Stevie Spring's story also reminded me of an ancient, famous, article on leadership in the *Harvard Business Review*, by Abraham Zaleznik. Usually, articles about the characteristics of a good leader or CEO make me feel skeptical, sometimes even nauseous. It always strikes me, when I look into the history of a company and analyze its strategic development, that it seems to need top people with widely different characteristics at different points in time. There is no one type of leader that everyone should aspire to.

Take my favourite little British company; the model-train maker Hornby. When it was in trouble about ten years ago, its board appointed a tough guy, Peter Newey. He slashed costs, rigorously made cuts in their portfolio and fired a bunch of people. He wasn't the most popular guy on the block (he was wise enough not to live in the company's home town Margate; he might have ended up with a knife in his back) but – with hindsight – people also respected him: he was what the company needed at the time, and it is doubtful it would have survived without him.

But then Hornby hired a people guy: Frank Martin. The first thing employees told me about him was: "he is extremely good at managing relationships" (something Newey wasn't exactly renowned for; and that's a euphemism). And he was; he built superb relationships with suppliers, customers, retailers, and investors. And the company flourished.

Yet, could he have done the tough turnaround job? Doubtful. He simply has other qualities. He too was the right man for the job at the time – just like Newey was.

You see the same thing at companies over and over again. Take Apple; in its early days, the energetic and charismatic Steve Jobs was exactly what the spawning company needed. However, when down-to-earth CEO John Sculley took over (much to the chagrin of Jobs), the company had one of its most profitable runs ever; Sculley didn't innovate, inspire bold new moves, or initiate great change; he focused on making money, and did that very well.

And that is what Apple needed at that point in time. Later, when it needed to be pushed and driven into a new direction, Sculley could not give it one; it was Jobs' time again, to inspire, initiate, and make the company grow. And again he did that very well. The same happened at the famous Swiss watch-maker Swatch: Ernest Thomke created the organization that led to the emergence of the innovative Swatch; subsequent CEO Nicolas Hayek took the invention and relentlessly managed the organization into a long streak of dominance and profitability. There is not one type of leader that fits all; different companies, at different times, need different people.

In the classic *Harvard Business Review* article "Managers and leaders: Are they different?" author Abraham Zaleznik's answer to this intriguing (and slightly provocative) question was an unambiguous "yes". Leaders inspire, are emotional, if not neurotic, and they are born that way. Managers are very different; they are rational, balanced, unemotional, and easy to get along with (although perhaps slightly boring). And it is not that one is superior to the other; different firms, at different stages of their development, need someone who inspires and does extraordinary things. But at other times, you need someone rational and objective, and perhaps slightly boring. Such a person may never be a "leader", but he can be a darn good manager.

Sometimes we need to be inspired, take risks, and dream up wacky things. Sometimes not. Banks come to mind. Sometimes, there is nothing wrong with a boring banker. Or a boring politician.

Women on top

Let me end this chapter with another speculative thought, one based on my own personal observations, about female CEOs.

In general, CEOs seem just like normal people. Some of them are nice, some of them unpleasant; some of them are modest, others are nauseatingly self-obsessed; some of them are bright, others more mentally challenged; some of them are helpful, others are cynically egotistic (and I could give you examples of each of these). Most of them are quite rich though ... And most of them are men.

Yet, over the years, I have also interviewed quite a few female CEOs: Barbara Cassani when she, way back when, was the CEO of Go Airlines (later acquired by easyJet), Sly Bailey, when she was still CEO of IPC Media (she is now the CEO of the newspaper group Trinity Mirror), Gail Rebuck, CEO of the book publisher Random House (who confirmed the famous rumor that she signed a big contract when she was in hospital giving birth) and, recently, Stevie Spring, CEO of magazine publisher Future, and Ruby McGregor-Smith, CEO of the large property services company MITIE. And they are all so nice!

I mean, really. Not nice as in bringing me cookies and pinching my cheek, but nice as in helpful, realistic, sympathetic, and down-to-earth. And bright. I have never met a dumb female CEO.

And I wonder why that is. I mean, it's just not normal.

My guess is the following: ascending to the position of CEO is a bit of a Darwinian process; many people start at the bottom of the corporate ladder, but very few reach the highest step. Climbing the ladder, as a woman, you still need something extra – especially when heading a public company, having to deal with the City (London's financial district) – at every step. And I guess that something extra is brains and tact (a fairly rare combination, also among professors by the way). Without brains or tact (or both), men can apparently still navigate and survive the corporate jungle. But women without brains or tact are "selected out" quite quickly. Therefore, when you see a woman step up, she is bound to be good!

Don't get me wrong, I have also met male CEOs who are "nice", as in helpful, realistic, sympathetic, and down-to-earth. And pretty much all female CEOs whom I interviewed displayed the attitude, "Stop whining about it being so difficult for women; just get on with it", but they also confirmed that they felt they needed something extra at every step of the way. I am not advocating that we should make it easier for women to reach the top and become CEOs, because that would mean that we'd get more CEOs who are unpleasant, nauseatingly self-obsessed, mentally challenged, and cynically egotistic. It is just that, perhaps, in corporate life, we should treat men more like we treat women. Wouldn't that be "nice"?

5

Liaisons and intrigues

Facts over fiction

This chapter, on liaisons and intrigues in business society, is suspiciously long. That's because there is quite a lot of it. Of course, rumors and dubiously founded accusations abound in the business world. In contrast, this chapter relies heavily on solid evidence: studies that carefully measure the existence of conflicts of interest, the exact causes and consequences of (excessive) remuneration, and the influence of who-knows-who in business.

It takes aim at three topics: the global phenomenon of investment banks and their analysts, boards of directors, and issues of top management team compensation. I will feed you facts about these three protagonists in a piecemeal fashion. As with any good soap opera, these pieces can be enjoyed on a stand-alone basis, but will add up to a coherent picture.

How influential are these equity analysts? How do banks handle potential conflicts of interest (if at all)? How are new board members selected? This chapter provides insights into the origins of excessive top management compensation, debunks the myth of stock options, and unveils the secret practices of the old boys' network (a.k.a boards of directors).

It may feel like a trashy novel, but it ain't no fiction.

Analysts, astrologers, and lemmings – three of a kind?

"Financial forecasting appears to be a science that makes astrology respectable," Burton Malkiel, Professor of Economics at Princeton, once said.

As you know, analysts, employed by investment banks, follow a number of firms (usually in a particular industry), evaluate them, and offer us recommendations, in terms of buy, sell, or hold on whether we should invest in their shares.

However, on average, these analysts give advice to sell in under 5 percent of cases. Yet, clearly, more than 5 percent of listed companies' share prices go down. So what's going on?

Well, there are various explanations, but one is that, for various reasons (pertaining to incentives in investment banks), analysts are inclined to cover firms whose share price they expect to go up. Therefore, perhaps an even more important decision than whether to recommend buy, sell or hold is the decision of which firms to cover.

And this is where it gets tricky (and almost a self-fulfilling prophecy). Research has shown that the stock price of firms goes up when they gain analyst coverage. That is, purely the fact that a research department (employing the analyst) decides to start covering the firm will increase its share price, probably simply because the firm becomes more well-known, is exposed to additional investors, which enables it to raise capital more easily, and so forth.

❝ Research has shown that the stock price of firms goes up when they gain analyst coverage. ❞

But how do research departments decide to start covering a firm? Well, research by Professors Huggy Rao, Henrich Greve, and Jerry Davis showed that this is very much influenced by imitation. They analyzed 1,442 firms listed on the NASDAQ stock market and the analysts covering them and, through elaborate statistical analysis, showed strong evidence that when one analyst starts covering a firm, his colleagues at other investment banks are inclined to start doing the same (irrespective of this firm's performance), thus creating a "cascade" of analyst coverage. Remember the residents of the Californian community discussed in Chapter 1 who all started conserving energy because everybody else was doing it – or so they thought? It seems analysts are the same: they follow the crowd, although they might not even realize it.

Subsequently, however, in their research project, Huggy and his colleagues also showed something else. Their models' findings revealed that, in such cascades, the imitating analysts were prone – more than usual – to overestimate the firm's future performance. And this made it very much a mixed blessing for the firm. Because analysts are inclined to cease coverage of companies which are underperforming in comparison to their predictions – which was very likely in this case, given the analysts' over-optimism – firms that initially benefited from increased analyst coverage were also more likely to suffer from analysts abandoning them.

The analysts, much like lemmings, jumped in, only to find out that the place they landed in wasn't as rosy as they had expected. This prompted them to jump out again, saving their skin, but leaving the firm trampled and bruised.

Conflicts of interest – do analysts rate their bank's clients' stock more favorably?

Have you ever heard that you can see the Great Wall of China from outer space? Well, it's a myth.

Have you ever heard of "Chinese walls" inside professional organizations, such as management consultants or solicitors, who face a potential conflict of interest, for instance, because some of their employees are working for different clients that compete in the same line of business? They claim they have "Chinese walls" inside their firms because their consultants or solicitors are not allowed to even talk to each other, let alone share information. Well, believe me, those are usually a myth as well.

Take investment banks. Investment banks often have a research department that employs analysts who provide recommendations on whether we should buy or sell the shares of a particular company. A recommendation to sell by such an analyst is quite a pain (in all sorts of body parts) for a company because their influence can be substantial, in the sense that the firm's share price will likely fall as a result of this recommendation. A recommendation to buy is obviously a much more cheerful event.

Such investments banks, however, often also have a corporate finance department which is trying to secure deals to advise companies on things like debt, equity, or M&A transactions. The potential conflict of interest is clear: if a bank's analyst gave a sell recommendation for a (potential) client company, this is going to be one valued client who is "not amused"!

Some companies are known to select only those investment banks to represent them on their deals who have awarded them positive stock recommendations in the past. In any case, if a bank is chatting up a client on the left side but recommending "sell their shares; now!" on the right side, this client might just tell them to f-off.

So how do investment banks deal with such potential conflicts of interest? "Chinese walls!" they'll so firmly declare that you will almost believe it. "We have Chinese walls in our firms, so that the corporate finance guys cannot pressure or even have lunch with the security analyst dudes". Yeah, right ...

Professors Mathew Hayward and Warren Boeker – at the time based at the London Business School – investigated exactly this issue. They selected 70 companies from a variety of industries (e.g., biotech, oil and gas, restaurants, telecom), collected a total of 8,169 analyst ratings that had been issued for them, and analyzed the investment banks that had been involved in their equity, debt, and M&A deals. Then they statistically examined whether analysts made more positive recommendations for those firms who their banks were also serving as clients. The answer was "heck, yes"; in 80 percent of the cases, analysts would rate

> **in 80 percent of cases, analysts would rate a company higher than their peers at other investment banks if this firm was also a client**

a company higher than their peers at other investment banks if this firm was also a client.

This was true when the rating was issued before the deal – at a time when the bank's corporate finance department was likely bidding or at least eyeing up a potential client – but also after a deal had been awarded, when the company was now officially a customer, and apparently able to exercise power. However, the closer the issue date of the rating to the deal date, and the larger the client, the stronger this influence was.

While the Great Wall of China might have been helpful at keeping the Hun tribes out of China, the mythical Chinese walls inside our professional corporations are apparently much worse at curtailing the influence of powerful stakeholders. Their presence can be measured and felt – at the end of the day, all the way into their shareholders' pockets.

Banks' blurry categorizations – have your cake and eat it too

"Animals are divided into (a) those that belong to the Emperor, (b) embalmed ones, (c) those that are trained, (d) suckling pigs, (e) mermaids, (f) fabulous ones, (g) stray dogs, (h) those that are included in this classification, (i) those that tremble as if they were mad, (j) innumerable ones, (k) those drawn with a very fine camel's hair brush, (l) others, (m) those that have just broken a flower vase, and (n) those that from a long way off look like flies."

This categorization was quoted by Jorge Borges in his book *Other Inquisitions*, from an ancient Chinese encyclopedia. I'm glad that in the world of business, when it comes to analyst recommendations whether to buy, sell or hold the shares of certain companies, we use rather more unambiguous classifications, don't we! Or do we?

As I previously discussed, analysts often face a potential conflict of interest. In principle, they are expected to offer solid and impartial advice on whether they think it's worth buying the shares of a particular company (because they forecast that the share price will go up) or whether they think it is time to offload any stock you bought in the past (because they forecast that its price will go down). However, their employer – the investment bank – quite often also serves this company as a client, for instance to advise them on their M&A, equity, and debt deals. The tricky thing is, companies don't like it (and this is a euphemism) when their own investment bank issues a negative (i.e., "sell") recommendation for their shares.

So, how do investment banks deal with this? As discussed, in the past, they often simply didn't. They would shamelessly issue a buy recommendation for a company just to secure it as a client. However, lately, this has become more and more tricky for a bank, to say the least. That's because the truth can eventually come out (we've seen examples of informal e-mail exchanges between bank employees in which they mock clients who they formally recommended to buy), but also because brokerage watchdogs have become focused on such behavior. More than ever, banks' long-term reputations can suffer if they make recommendations (e.g., buy) which later turn out to be quite wrong, loss-making, or plain stupid.

So, how do banks resolve this tricky dilemma? Anne Fleischer – an assistant professor at the University of Toronto – undertook an intriguing piece of analysis. She looked at ambiguity in banks' equity ratings systems and how it was related to such conflicts of interest.

You have to realize that banks use different classification schemes in their advice regarding the attractiveness of certain stocks, and these vary in terms of how ambiguous they can be. For example, buy; sell; hold is simple enough isn't it? But many firms use five categories, including a strong buy and clear sell. Still pretty unambiguous, right? But what about "buy/high risk" versus "buy/low risk"; a bit trickier, no? Or "buy; positive; hold; neutral; negative"? Or what about the difference between "buy" and "accumulate" (also found within one and the same classification scheme)?! Some banks have up to 16 different categories, advising us to buy or not. But why would they create such opaque, blurry schemes to advise us in the first place?

Might it have anything to do with covering their back when they face a conflict of interest...? Could it perhaps enable them to get away with not offering unambiguous sell advice on a client (risking pissing them off) while in reality their analysts are pessimistic about the company's prospects? After all, if they recommend an unambiguous buy but the share price plummets, they will look incompetent, if not worse. However, what if they had recommended us a "speculative buy"? Guess that might divert the blame a bit and get them off the hook. Perhaps such ambiguous schemes help banks make blurry recommendations that keep both angry investors and overbearing clients at bay? Would banks really be that devious?

Anne didn't just think; she looked at the facts. She had some financial specialists rate how ambiguous the rating schemes were of 207 brokerage firms. Then she computed to what extent these firms faced a potential conflict of interest, because they were both providing purchase advice and securing the same companies as clients underwriting their debt and equity offerings or supporting their M&A activity. The results were clear: those investment banks that faced a conflict of interest developed more ambiguous classification schemes to "advise" us on the purchase and sale of company shares.

" sometimes banks don't want to create clarity at all "

Evidently, these equity rating systems are not just created with the aims of unequivocal advice and clarity in mind. Quite the contrary; sometimes banks don't want to create clarity at all. Blurring the boundaries helps them cover their tracks, make money on both sides of the table, and thus have their cake and eat it too.

Analysts rule the waves (whether we like it or not)

I will briefly return to the topic of conflicts of interest a little later, but let me now elaborate a bit on the influence of equity analysts. Their influence on a firm's stock price is known to be substantial, as one would expect from a financial analyst. Thus, they determine the amount of financial resources available to a firm. However, their impact actually goes quite a bit further than that: because of their power to determine a company's access to financial means, they also have a substantial influence on what sort of strategy the firm is pursuing in the first place. A good setting to illustrate this is corporate diversification.

In the 1960s we saw a wave of "diversification" among corporations, resulting in the emergence of many so-called conglomerates. They operated in all sorts of businesses that often didn't have much to do with each other. For example, a famous conglomerate in the UK was Hanson plc, whose divisions operated in activities ranging from chemical factories to electrical suppliers, gold mines, cigarettes, batteries, airport duty-free stores, clothing shops, and department stores. Diversification was popular and conglomerates flourished.

In the 1990s though, the trend reversed, and we witnessed a wave of de-diversification. Firms started to focus on their "core activities", companies were split up, conglomerates were dismantled, and diversification was generally regarded as unfashionable, evil, and simply not done.

What led the trend to reverse? Economists have argued that it was shareholders fighting back. Shareholders can diversify their stock portfolios; they don't need companies to do that for them. Managers only do so to serve their own needs, and feed their desire for empire-building, size, and security. In the 1990s, shareholders said "basta" and forced self-serving managers to de-diversify – or so they claim.

A slightly kinder view is offered by sociologists, who argue that in the 1960s it was considered good practice to spread risk and diversify and hence a "legitimate thing to do". Managers weren't selfish and evil; they simply did what was expected of them. When shareholders said, "We don't want you to do this anymore" (perhaps because the market became more transparent and efficient), they diligently responded and applied more focus to their companies.

Yet, more recently, researchers have started to focus on the role that analysts played and still play in discouraging companies to spread their activities across different industries. After all, sometimes diversification might make sense! For example, a company like Monsanto sort of had to operate in pharmaceuticals, agricultural chemicals, and agricultural biotechnology because its expertise bridged these different areas and therefore it was advantageous to operate in all of them. But that something makes sense from a strategy perspective doesn't mean it makes sense in light of an analyst's lunch-break.

What do analysts' lunch-breaks have to do with any of this, you might wonder.

Well ... it is very important for listed firms to be covered by analysts. We know from ample research that firms who receive less coverage usually trade at a significantly lower share price. Consider this quote, from an analyst report by PaineWebber in 1999:

"The life sciences experiment is not working with respect to our analysis or in reality. Proper analysis of Monsanto requires expertise in three industries: pharmaceutical, agricultural chemicals, and agricultural biotechnology. Unfortunately, on Wall Street, these separate industries are analyzed individually because of the complexity of each. At PaineWebber, collaboration among analysts brings together expertise in each area. We can attest to the challenges of making this effort pay off: just co-ordinating a simple thing like work schedules requires lots of effort. While we are willing to pay the price that will make the process work, it is a process not likely to be adopted by Wall Street on a widespread basis. Therefore, Monsanto will probably have to change its structure to be more properly analyzed and valued."*

Wait a second, did they just suggest that Monsanto should split up because it requires three (industry-specific) analysts to cover them and these three jokers can't find a mutually convenient time to meet?! Yes, I am afraid they did.

---

* Adapted with permission from by *Corporate Strategy, Analyst Coverage, and the Uniqueness Paradox* by Litov, Moreton, and Zenger, Washington University at St Louis. See http://papers.ssrn.com/.sol3/papers.cfm?abstract id=1364037#http://paper.ssrn.com/sol3/papers.cfm?abstract id=1364037

Along similar lines, in a large research project, Ezra Zuckerman, Professor at MIT, found that firms divested businesses, split up, or demerged in order to make themselves easier to understand for analysts. Those firms who, for one reason or another, comprised an unusual combination of businesses in their corporation and therefore were "more difficult to understand" for the poor analysts traded at a significantly lower price. They could try to explain their strategy at length but after a while the only thing left for them to do was to split it. Arthur Stromberg, then CEO of URS Corporation, who initiated its spin-off, declared: "I realized that analysts are like the rest of us. Give them something easy to understand, and they will go with it. [Before the spin-off,] we had made it tough for them to figure us out."

Security analysts usually specialize in one or a specific combination of industries. If a firm does not conform to that division of analyst labor, it is more difficult to understand and analyse, which is why it will trade at a lower price. It then makes sense to give in to the analysts' whims, and focus and simplify, even if that would make you weaker in a strictly business sense. Hence, analysts rule the (diversification) waves. And their lunch-break will determine your stock price.

66 analysts rule the (diversification) waves 99

Sirens and investment bankers – birds of a feather

As I have discussed so far, analysts have a substantial influence on a firm's stock price, therefore on its access to financial resources, and therefore on what strategies managers decide to pursue. In addition, they face a conflict of interest, because they are rating firms that are often also their banks' (prospective) customers. I would say that these conflicts of interests go a bit further, and are not restricted only to banks' analysts. With it, banks' influence on firms' strategies go further than often realized. Let me return, as an example, to the now familiar topic of acquisitions.

Some time ago, I was interviewing a CEO of a FTSE 100 company, which had acquired dozens of companies over the past years, when we came to speak about investment bankers. He then asked me, "Do you know who the Sirens were, in Greek mythology?" I said "yes" (because I did and, of course, also because I did not want to appear ignorant).

Sirens were beautiful maidens located on a small island surrounded by cliffs and rocks. They would lure seamen who sailed near the island with their enchanting singing, to shipwreck them on the rocks.

"Well," this CEO continued, "investment bankers are just like Sirens." That caught my attention. "How's that?" I asked. "They constantly try to seduce you into doing another deal, and they don't care at all whether that deal actually make sense for the company. It's like they are trying to make you shipwreck onto the rocks for their own benefit," he said. OK … that's one (slightly peculiar) way to describe your own advisors …

Of course, he does have a point: firms and their shareholders are not the only parties potentially benefiting from a transaction. A vast industry exists that initiates, values, negotiates, and closes deals. However, the interests of such parties, for instance investment bankers, may not always be aligned with those of the firm. Especially when M&A times are relatively slow, investment bankers may attempt to initiate deals from which it is not clear that they are to the benefit of the potential acquirer.

As an ex-investment banker told me some time ago, "When times were slow, we'd all go through our address books and discuss 'who hasn't done a deal for a long time', because we would usually be able to talk such a person into doing one."

Yet, one could – if one really wanted to – make a good argument that investment bankers are not necessarily to blame for this; they are supposed to follow their interests and it is up to the manager to say "no" to a proposed transaction.

Yet, deals – and investment bankers – can be seductive. Sometimes, CEOs who are inclined to at least listen to their investment bank would do well to do like Odysseus; Odysseus wanted to hear the mythical Sirens sing but was less keen on shipwrecking. So he asked his sailors to plug their ears with beeswax and to tie him firmly to the ship's mast. They then sailed past the Sirens; Odysseus was overwhelmed by their music but, being restrained, could not free himself to follow his urges and run his ship onto the rocks.

All we need now are boards with beeswax and offices with a mast. I can bring the rope.

How to tame an analyst

Let's face it; analysts are a very strange phenomenon in our global economy. The previous pages show some examples. These people advise us to buy, sell, or hold particular companies' stock but we also all know that the banks that employ them make money if we buy. More importantly, we know that these very same companies that they advise us on are the banks' customers (e.g., for their M&A deals), which makes it a rather hefty conflict of interest (especially when the real advice should be "sell, now!"). Moreover, on what information do these analysts base their recommendations? (1) The same oh-so-reliable numbers as the rest of us have too, and (2) talking to the company's sweet-talking CEO. Oooh ... that's comforting ...

It is of course a nice, glamorous perk for the average analyst; being invited to personal audiences with a real-life CEO. Mind you, though, if you subsequently don't write nicely about their company, they won't invite you back! That'll teach you!

Or do you think I am exaggerating, and starting to create a parody of what is a very serious financial business? Well, let me tell you a story. And it is a story about facts.

Professor Jim Westphal from the University of Michigan and Michael Clement from the University of Texas at Austin examined this issue: the relationship between CEOs and analysts. They surveyed a total of 4,595 American analysts and examined the strategies and performance of the companies they made recommendations on.

In the surveys, they asked the analysts to what extent they had been given the privilege of personal access to certain top executives, in the form of private meetings, returned phone calls or conference calls, and so on, and how often this form of individual access was denied. They also asked them about personal favors that these CEOs might have done for them, such as putting them in contact with the manager of another company, recommending them for a position, or giving advice on personal or career matters. Then Jim and Mike ran some numbers.

First of all, their statistical models showed that the CEOs of companies that had to announce relatively low corporate earnings started to significantly increase the number of favors they handed out to analysts, by granting them personal meetings, jovially returning their phone calls, and making some much-appreciated introductions. Similarly, CEOs of companies that were about to engage in diversifying acquisitions – a controversial if not dubious strategy that the stock market invariably hates – engaged in much the same thing. Clearly, these CEOs were trying to sweet-talk the analysts and mellow the mood ahead of some rather disappointing announcements they were about to make. The question is: did it work?

What do you think? Is the Pope Catholic? Is Steve Jobs whizzier than MacGyver? Did Neutron Jack eat all his meat?! Is Bill Clinton heterosexual?!?! Sorry, don't let me get carried away in analogy here; the answer is yes.

Of course it's yes. It works. Analysts who received more personal favors from a CEO would rate a company's stock more positively when he announced disappointing results or engaged in questionable strategies. And if they didn't? Yep, you guessed it: those analysts who, in spite of the favors, had the indignity of downgrading the company's stock all of a sudden ceased to have their phone

> ££ Analysts who received more personal favors from a CEO would rate a company's stock more positively ᛋᛋ

calls returned, would be denied any further personal meetings, and sure as hell were not given the phone number of the CEO's golfing buddies. And the only advice they ever received was to get a life and bend their bodies in ways that would enable self-fertilization.

And this worked too (not the self-fertilization bit, but the social punishment). Other analysts aware of their colleagues' plight and loss of status would be sure to not follow them into the social abyss; they were unlikely to downgrade the firm of the proven-to-be-vindictive CEO. Thus, analysts let themselves be significantly influenced by the CEOs of the companies they were supposed to rate objectively.

And what might CEOs pick up from this? Well, all in all, it shows that sweet-talking works. But mostly if followed by a good dose of old-fashioned bullying.

Advice or influence? Why firms ask government officials to be directors

Let's face it; outside directors are a strange phenomenon in our global economy. Analysts may be peculiar, but boards of directors certainly seem to be a governance construction that is stranger than fiction. Because they are a bunch of amateurs and part-timers. Literally. Sometimes these directors are not even business people, but unionists or politicians. Moreover, the supervision of the management of a globally diversified company is just something they do on the side – a couple of days per year or so. Often they are CEOs of other companies – so that might help a bit (or harm a bit ...) – but typically these guys have about half a dozen of these gigs. So, they can't let any single one of them distract them too much.

It is a bit like we manage our own personal finances – paying bills and filing bank statements and so forth. In the evening, after a hard day's work, while watching *X Factor*, we quickly glance over the financials and put our signature on the most necessary evils before making a cup of coffee and turning our attention to the newspaper. Bills, bank statements, the accounts of a multinational; what's the difference really?

But, as I said, not all outside directors are (ex-)CEOs. Quite often, companies also invite ex-government officials to serve on their boards. The reasons for that, as research has indicated, are not hard to fathom: they can provide advice, but they can also provide influence. I guess there's nothing wrong with buying advice, but the idea of buying influence might be a bit more morally challenged ...

Government officials can provide specific advice on how to deal with government-related issues. They have specific knowledge and experience and can therefore provide valuable advice. But ex-officials can also offer contacts for communication that are not accessible to other companies. Then, directorships start to become the currency used to buy influence, which makes it a bit more dubious. It certainly gets dubious if they provide a direct way to influence political decisions. Some people have even suggested that board memberships for ex-government officials are rewards for services rendered while they were in government ... which would certainly be in the "barely legal" category.

It's hard to examine which of the aforementioned reasons motivates firms to invite ex-government officials on to their board: the legal ones (e.g., specialist advice) or the barely legal ones (influence and rewards for past services). However, by analyzing which individuals are offered the job, we can get a sense of what's going on. Professor Richard Lester from Texas A&M University and some of his colleagues analyzed this question: which government officials are most likely to be approached to serve on a board? Using data from the US, they tracked all senators, congressmen, and presidential cabinet ministers who left office between 1988 and 2003 and figured out which of them were offered directorships.

They found that the longer officials had served in government, the more likely they were to be approached for a directorship. I guess that could be because more experience gives them more influence, but also because experience made them better advisors.

So no verdict here just yet. Presidential cabinet ministers were more likely to receive board invites than senators, who were more likely to be approached than congressmen. I think this starts to lean towards an "influence" explanation for board invites rather than an "advice" one, but if you'd really like to jump to their defense I guess one could still argue that cabinet ministers simply might make for better advisors.

However, another clear finding was that these people would either get asked for a board very shortly after leaving their government position, or not at all. Senators and former cabinet officers would usually be snapped up in the first year after leaving office. This could hardly be because after a year they would suddenly make lousy advisors; it's much more consistent with the fact that their ability to influence government decisions quickly deteriorates after leaving office. And it seems consistent with the idea that they get offered the job in return for services already delivered ...

Finally, Richard and colleagues examined what happened in the case of a government change; that is, if the party in power (in the House, the Senate, or the White House) shifted from Democrat to Republican or vice versa. The effect of this was clear; the ex-government official, associated with the party no longer in power, would see his invites dry up rapidly. He had just lost his attraction as a potential board member, because if the wrong party comes to power, you see your power to influence evaporate and, with it, your value as a potential board member. Clearly this points at an "influence" argument; companies ask ex-government officials on their boards to bend political decisions in their favor. And I'm afraid this puts these officials firmly in the "barely legal" category.

Boards of directors: cliques and elites

Let me entertain you a bit more in the shady world of boards of directors. And show you how they form a business elite that operates as a self-governing clique.

In the US, in the 1980s, shareholders (especially institutional investors) began to advocate that company directors should take certain measures that restrict top managers from having a ball at shareholders' expense: that is, undertake strategic actions that are in their own interest but not in those of the company's shareholders. Yet, after making some initial inroads, two decades later, this reform process stagnated. For example, the portion of large US companies with an independent board chair or an independent nominating committee for new board members (two of the things advocated by the investors) was only slightly higher in 1999 than in 1989.

How come? Why had this governance reform stagnated? To answer this question, Professor James Westphal – currently at the University of Michigan – conducted an elaborate study. He collected data on 417 firms, interviewed scores of top managers and directors, obtained surveys from 1,098 directors and 197 CEOs at multiple points in time, and came up with an intriguing answer. He found that the top managers and board members of the US's biggest companies together form an "elite", which acts very much like "the clique of popular kids in high school". Let me explain.

Specifically, Jim tracked directors' voting behavior when any of the following four measures were being proposed in the company (which each limit top managers' power):

1 CEOs cannot concurrently also hold the seat of chairman of the board (so that the board can operate independently).

2 The company should have a nominating committee to appoint new board members, rather than the company's CEO controling this process.

3 The director at some point had voted to dismiss the (underperforming) company's CEO (a measure clearly not in the interest of the CEO!).

4 The company should revoke a so-called poison-pill construction – a mechanism that makes it difficult for a firm to be acquired against top management's will (so that even when top management is doing a poor job, and the company is underperforming, they still can't be ousted by new owners).

Then, Jim examined what had happened to the directors that had voted in favor of adopting one or more of these ("controversial") measures ...

First, what you have to realize is that people who hold board memberships are also often members of the boards of other companies. If a particular board member, at some point in time, had voted for one of the above measures, which remove privileges from top managers (i.e., members of the elite) and give them to investors (who are not considered part of the elite), their fellow directors at other boards would subsequently start to give them the cold shoulder. The board member would become unpopular with the rest of the in-crowd, and be treated as a traitor.

The questionnaires and interviews (conducted with both the "unpopular board members" themselves as well as with their former "friends") clearly indicated that the other board members would start to engage in subtle behavior intended to punish the deviant person, such as neglecting to invite him to an informal meeting, not asking his opinion or advice in formal meetings, not acknowledging or building on his comments in discussion, engaging in exclusionary gossip whereby they would talk about other people and events with which the director was not familiar, and so on. Basically the good old pretend-you're-not-there kind of stuff.

For example, board members said that the deviant persons "can expect to be ostracized", and "people are less interested in working with them". One director said, "The directors [who had voted for one of the four changes] get treated differently – I think they get put on notice a bit", while another commented, "It will hurt you. You won't get thrown off the board, but you definitely won't get treated the same. In a way you get treated like the enemy – or at least a suspect". One director, who had once voted in favor of one of the measures, related his own experience: "After we fired the CEO I got the cold shoulder from colleagues at another board ... I didn't get invited to an important meeting."

Does this perhaps remind you of your high-school days...? Water in your locker, a "kick me" sign on your back, your school books thrown in the bin, your clothes vanished when you returned from the gymnasium shower? That's the faith and reality of a deviant board member, who went against the wishes of the elite.

And, guess what, it worked. Jim, in his statistical analysis, also examined the subsequent voting behavior of the directors who had been subject to such treatment. Whenever, in the ensuing years, there was another vote on one of the four aforementioned measures, the directors would cave in, and vote against it. He didn't dare do it again.

"Relax, gentlemen. There are more
chairs in the next room."

Board-cloning – a rewarding habit

Who do CEOs think should succeed them? Well, someone like them of course.

But then, who do their boards think should succeed the CEO? Well, someone who is much more like the members of the board, of course.

Then, what does the CEO think the next board member should ideally look like? Well, someone quite like him of course.

Does the current board agree with this? No, usually not; they think the new board member should be much more like them.

This sums up the research that Professors James Westphal and Ed Zajac (at the time both at Northwestern University) did in the mid-1990s on CEO successors and the background characteristics of newly appointed board members. Surprising it is not – we all like people who are like us, and think that they are so much more competent than the next guy – but I still find it striking (if not shocking) how Jim and Ed could so easily uncover evidence of these tendencies using a few simple statistics.

They measured some straightforward background characteristics of all of these guys (sorry ... yes, usually guys), such as their age, their functional background, education, etc., in 413 Fortune 500 companies. Using these measures, they computed how dissimilar newly appointed CEOs and board members were from the prior CEO and from existing board members.

If the incumbent CEO was in a powerful position (because he was both CEO and chairman of the board, had long tenure, the firm had been performing relatively well, and because there were few outside directors on the board, who owned little stock), incoming CEOs and board members would be much more like the previous CEO – obviously this guy used his powerful position to make sure someone was selected who could be mistaken for his clone. Yet, the reverse was true too; if the board members had more power, they would select someone quite unlike the CEO and much more similar to themselves.

The tricky thing is of course when the CEO succeeds in selecting more and more board members who are just like him. Then the process escalates because board members and the CEO start liking the same people! Eventually, everyone in the firm starts to look alike, talk alike, has the same background, education, taste in cars, dress, entertainment, and so on and so on. Sounds familiar? Know any companies like that? Perhaps you're employed by a firm just like that (and there's a good chance that you fit in nicely), or perhaps it reminds you of the phenomenon of "the success trap", or perhaps – and even worse – both!

Interestingly, Jim and Ed also analyzed what happened to the compensation packages that firms offered to their CEO, if the CEO succeeded in selecting more and more people like them. Guess what? The percentage of his pay that was performance-related went down, while the total amount of his compensation went up!

I guess CEOs don't just like and select people who are just like them, but those people quite like our CEO too! And reward him handsomely for it. After all, from their perspective, obviously, "he does have the most amazing background credentials".

Boardroom friends

Lately, of course, boards of directors in various countries and systems have been subject to considerable frowning, loathing, smirking, and indecent hand gestures. "They're all part of the same elite", "corporate amateurs", "never really objective", "not really independent", "an old-boys' network", and so on. Surely, it is said, those directors that are pretty much personal friends of the CEO will be most useless; they will just protect him and never really be critical, asking the nasty and awkward questions they should be asking.

Yet, is this necessarily so? Do "friends" make for bad directors? Professor James Westphal, of the University of Michigan (yes, him again), became skeptical of the skeptics. He investigated whether social relations between board members and CEOs really are as harmful as assumed. He extensively surveyed 243 CEOs and 564 of their outside directors and examined whether personal friendships and acquaintances made for less effective board members.

First of all, he found that the boardroom friends hardly ever engaged in less "monitoring" of the CEO (that is, checking strategic decisions, formal performance evaluation, etc.) – the traditional stuff that directors are supposed to do. They were still quite active in that sense, despite being a personal friend of the CEO.

In addition, Jim found that boardroom friends engaged a lot in another type of behavior towards the CEO: ongoing advice and counseling. They gave their CEO informal feedback about the formulation of the firm's strategy: they acted as a 'sounding board', continuously provided general feedback and suggestions, etc. All this happened outside the company's formal board meetings. Directors who were not personal friends hardly engaged in this type of behavior.

Usually CEOs don't easily do this; accept or even ask for ongoing counselling and opinion. It is well known from research that a primary inhibitor to seeking advice is the perceived effect it could have on the advice-seeker's status. People often believe that others will view their need for assistance as an admission of uncertainty or dependency, and as an indication that they are less than fully competent or self-reliant.

❝ having your friends in the boardroom may not be such a bad thing after all ❞

There is little doubt that CEOs – who are expected to be confident, proud, and self-assured – have these tendencies too! Fierce, testosterone-driven CEOs may not take criticism or even advice easily, but if the director is a personal friend, it might be easier to swallow. Psychologically, it is easier to listen to criticism from someone you know and trust than from a stranger. Hence, having your friends in the boardroom may not be such a bad thing after all.

CEOs and their stock options … (oh please …)

Let me now turn my attention (and hopefully yours too …) to the topic of how CEOs generally are rewarded by their boards. And a major element here is, of course, the illustrious stock options. Any idea why we continue to reward top executives with stock options? We accept it, nowadays, as a given, but why do we have that practice in the first place?

You might say "because it constitutes performance-related pay; through them, you financially reward top managers for their achievements". Fair enough, because for many of us mortals our pay depends to some extent on our performance. However, do realize that for CEOs, for example, this component is often as high as 80 percent. Eighty percent! Do you know many people (employed in the same large corporations that these executives head) whose salary is 80-percent dependent on some measure of their achievements? Not many I suspect.

And, in theory, large corporations that reward their top managers through stock are right – and I am saying "in theory" for a reason. This practice – of offering CEOs stock-based pay – is a recommendation straight out of something called "agency theory". It is one of the few scientific theories in management academia that has actually influenced the world of management practice. It is basically a theory that stems from economics. It says that you have to align the interests of the people managing the firm (top executives) with those of its shareholders, otherwise they will only do things that are in their own interest, will be inactive, lazy, or plain deceitful. Yep, these economists have an uplifting world-view. But that is why we have such a huge performance-related component in the pay of most top executives.

But are you really sure you want people like that managing your firm? People who will be lazy and purely operate in their own interest if given a chance? Do you really want a CEO who really needs performance-related pay and who otherwise, if put on a fixed salary, wouldn't do much and just hang about? In case you missed it, I intended this as a rhetorical question ...

But anyway, we give them stock – and lots of it – to incentivize them. But the question still lingers: why stock *options*? And that's a story in itself.

Agency theory doesn't only say that people will be lazy and deceitful if given a chance; it also says that managers are inherently risk-averse; much more risk-averse than shareholders would like them to be. And the theory prescribes that you should give them stock options, rather than stock, to stimulate them to take more risk.

"More risk!?" you might think. Do we really want CEOs of large corporations to take *more* risk?! Is it not, given recent events in the world of business, that we would like our top executives to be a little less risk-taking for a change? Ah, that's what you might think now, but it is not what agency theory thinks, and it is not what the incentive structure of most public corporations nowadays is geared to do.

Because stock options do stimulate risk-seeking behavior, as we know from scientific research. Options, as you might know, represent a right to buy shares at a certain price at some fixed point in the future. If you are given the right to buy a share in company X for $100 in January 2010 and by then the share price of X is $120, you will make 20 bucks per share. However, if the company's share price by then has dropped to $90, your option is worthless; we say it is "out of the money": you're not going to exercise your right to buy at $100 when the market price is merely $90.

In that situation, if the CEO of X has many stock options, it stimulates him to be very risk-seeking. For example, if by August 2009 the share price is $90, he will be inclined to engage in risky "win or lose" moves. If the risk pays off and the share price rises well above $100, the stock options will become worth a lot of money. However, if he loses, and the share price plummets even further, say to $60, it doesn't matter. The stock options to buy at $100 were worthless anyway, whether the stock trades at $90 or at $60.

But what sort of risk-taking does this really lead to? Because what agency theory has not really acknowledged and explored is that there are various types of risk. Some risks may be good; some are not so good … Are we sure that stock options lead to sensible risk-taking?

Stock options, risk, and manipulations

No, I am not so sure. Two strategy professors have actually measured this: Gerry Sanders from Rice University and Don

Hambrick from Penn State University. They examined 950 American CEOs, their stock options and their risk-taking behavior. They found that CEOs with many stock options made much bigger bets: for instance, they would do more and larger acquisitions, bigger capital investments, and higher R&D expenditures. That is, where CEOs with few stock options would prefer to invest $50 million in a particular project, they would plunge in $100 million.

However, in addition, they would bet (that rather substantial amount of) money on things that had much higher variability. That is, if there was a project that could make them win or lose 20 percent of the sum invested and another project that could make them win or lose 50 percent, they would pick the latter; big bets with lots of variance.

Yet, I guess those could still be regarded "good risks". Gerry and Don, however, also found something else: option-loaded CEOs delivered significantly more big losses than big gains! They would more often lose than win the big bets. Surely that is not something anyone would want.

And why is that? Well, through these stock options, you have created individuals at the helm of your firm who only care about the up-side, but can't be bothered with the size of the down-side; whether they lose $10 million or $100 million, their stock options are worthless anyway.

And it gets worse. Professor Xiaomeng Zhang and colleagues, from the American University in Washington, D.C., examined the relationship between stock options and earnings manipulations: plain illegal behavior. They investigated 365 earnings manipulation cases and showed that CEOs with many "out of the money" options were more likely to misrepresent their company's financial results (and get caught doing it!).

And I guess that's not something even the biggest risk-loving shareholder would applaud. Hence, even if as a board member or shareholder you'd want to stimulate your CEO to take more risks – and I guess that is a big *if* – I am not so sure that stock options will get you the kind of risk you're after. Stock options lead to risk-seeking behavior, but they're not always the risks you'd like CEOs to take.

Too hot to handle: explaining excessive top management remuneration

In many countries the topic of "excessive top management compensation" – especially for CEOs – triggers much emotion, social outcry, and even calls to arms for politicians to finally regulate the issue and introduce mandatory caps on salaries. And I used to think that this was all nonsense, because the high salaries of CEOs were simply the result of a market mechanism and "the way it is" (and certainly none of politicians' business). However, the more I learn about CEO compensation, through scientific research, and the workings of boards of directors (who usually determine a CEO's remuneration package) the more I realize there is more going on than that.

First of all, there has been quite a bit of research that has tried to show that CEO compensation is tied to firm performance. As it turns out, it ain't. That research has tried, has tried hard and harder, but just could not deliver much evidence of this. Admittedly, some studies have uncovered some minor positive relations between pay and performance, but it wasn't much. The salary of the average CEO seems completely disconnected from how well his firm is performing.

The only economic factor worth mentioning that has delivered some consistent results explaining top management remuneration – indicating a positive influence on CEO pay – is firm size: bigger firms pay better. Although this may be an intuitive result, it is actually not that clear why. Why do the CEOs of big firms earn more? Do CEOs of big firms put in more hours? Not that I know of. Is managing a **bigger firms pay better** firm with 100,000 employees that much harder and more demanding than managing a firm with a tenth of that number on their payroll? Not necessarily. So what is it? I guess one could argue that a top manager of a large firm can do more damage if he messes up and, since large firms generally have more resources available than smaller firms, they hire (and pay) the best. Yeah … I guess that could be it … Although research has also shown that, on average, large firms are not really more profitable than small ones, so I am not sure these better-paid guys actually are any better at their jobs. But anyway, we have found one thing that seems to explain top executive pay, so let's not be too critical about it but accept it with grace.

But, beyond plain size, what else determines CEO remuneration? Well, let's start with *who* determines CEO compensation. In most countries, for public firms, that'll be the board of directors. And, specifically, the directors that serve on the firm's remuneration committee (usually three to five outside directors). And, yes, there has been some research on these bozos.

Three professors who did research on the relation between CEO compensation and boards of directors were Charles O'Reilly and Graef Crystal from the University of California in Berkeley and Brian Main from the University of St Andrews in Scotland. They studied 105 large American companies and first computed the relation between a bunch of economic factors (such as firm performance and firm size) and CEO remuneration. The only thing they found was a connection between company sales and CEO pay. In short, on average, if a firm's sales increased by $100 million during the CEO's tenure, his salary would go up by $18,000. That's hardly impressive, now is it?

Then, Charles, Graef, and Brian did something a bit more interesting. You have to realize that the directors on these committees are usually CEOs or ex-CEOs themselves. Therefore, Charles and his colleagues compared the salaries of these director CEOs to the salaries of the CEOs of the companies for which they served on the remuneration committee. There was a strong relationship between them. An increment in the average salary of such an outside director, say, $100,000 was associated with a jump in salary of $51,000 for the CEO, after statistically correcting for all the results due to the effects of firm size, profitability, etc.! Charles, Graef, and Brian argued that this association could only be the result of some sort of psychological social comparison process. The directors on the remuneration committee who decide on the CEO's salary simply determine this guy's pay by looking at what they themselves make at their companies. And thus, doing this, they don't feel hindered by irrelevant issues such as the firm's actual performance during the tenure of the CEO or any other silly things like that!

And guess what, who do you think usually determines who is invited to serve as an outside director for a firm? Any guesses? Yep, it is generally a company's CEO who nominates new outside directors. But doesn't that make it rather tempting for CEOs to only nominate very highly paid peers to serve as directors on their boards? You might wonder. Yes … I guess it does …

The more highly paid the directors who you put on your board, the more handsomely they are likely to reward you!

Yes, the more highly paid the directors who you put on your board, the more handsomely they are likely to reward you! Thus, their wealth may nicely domino into your bank account. The last people you'd want on your board are those guys who are on a meager package themselves; because they would likely curb your dosh as well. Instead, bring in the rich guys; they'll make you rich too!

How to justify paying top managers too much

As I said, the level of top managers' compensation is often a contentious topic. Basically, most people think these guys get paid too much. They claim it's simply the result of the market mechanism, supply and demand: good managers are scarce and therefore they earn hefty salaries (like movie stars, football players and other demigods).

Although there is of course a bit of a market at work, it has to be said that the people who determine the pay of a company's CEO – the board of directors – do face a conflict of interest of sorts. Board memberships are nice jobs to have, in the sense that they are usually rather lucrative gigs and provide a pleasant dosage of power and prestige for those who get them. And – this is where the conflict of interest arises – as I explained in the previous section, it's mostly the company's top managers who nominate new board members. In the spirit of "don't bite the hand that just fed you", board members may be inclined to reward their benefactors (i.e., the CEO) handsomely by returning the favor in the form of a nice compensation package.

Moreover, as also discussed above, directors who deviate from this social norm (and for instance vote for a relatively low CEO compensation package) will be frowned upon by the rest of the business elite, spat at and given the cold shoulder until they "come to their senses" and change their ridiculous behavior.

For this reason, in various countries, boards of directors now have to justify the compensation packages they give to their CEOs by explicitly comparing the firm and its performance to a "peer group". The idea is that, due to this forced comparison, it becomes more difficult for boards to step out of line. The tricky thing is, of course, how do you determine a company's peer group?

It seems most logical to simply pick a group of firms in the company's main industry, right? Right – but even firms in the same industry are usually not entirely comparable: you have many different types of banks, pharmaceutical companies can be vastly dissimilar, software companies will not be alike, and one retailer is not identical to the next one. Therefore, boards have some flexibility regarding who to include in their firm's "peer group". And that's of course a rather tempting opportunity for a bit of old-fashioned manipulation ...

Professors Joe Porac, Jim Wade and Tim Pollock analyzed the composition of the peer groups chosen by the boards of 280 large American companies. For each peer group, they examined how many firms were in there that were not from the company's primary industry – thinking that there might be something fishy going on. Subsequently, they looked at the financial performance of the peer groups, of the companies in the sample, the performance of each company's industry, and the size of the CEOs' compensation packages.

They found that boards would usually construct peer groups consisting of firms in the company's primary industry. On average, there were some 30 percent of firms in those peer groups that weren't in a company's line of business. But, guess what: this figure increased significantly if the firm was performing poorly; then the board would construct a peer group of firms (outside the company's industry) with mediocre performance, to make the firm look better. They did the same thing if everybody in the company's industry was performing well; then a poorer-performing peer group obscured the fact that the good performance of the company was nothing unusual in its industry, again making it look comparatively good.

Finally, boards would compose peer groups that consisted of comparatively poorly performing firms from outside the company's industry if its CEO received a relatively hefty compensation package; then the seemingly high performance of the firm would come in handy to justify the CEO's big bucks.

Joe, Jim, and Tim concluded, "boards selectively define peers in self-protective ways".

Which simply means that they dupe us to pay the buggers too much.

CEOs do seek advice – if you pay them for it …

So, now we know that stock options alter top managers' behavior (in the form of risk-taking), but what about performance-related pay in general? Does this alter behavior in other ways too? And does it actually improve it?

I know I previously said that I find it a bit strange that top managers would need performance-related pay. Do you really want someone at the helm of your company if he only works hard and smart if he's directly rewarded for it? On the other hand, I have to admit, no matter how rhetorical this question is intended, I guess it is only human nature …

It is human that our behavior alters due to performance-related pay; and you and I are probably no exception. The trick then, of course, is to get the right measurement system, and perhaps not to overdo it; too much performance-related pay may alter the behavior of top executives in ways you had not got in mind when putting the measures in place! We've seen ample examples of that over recent years … Enron, Lehmann, and Worldcom come to mind.

So, how might it bias top executives' behavior in useful ways? Professors Michael McDonald from the University of Central Florida, Poonam Khanna from Arizona State University, and Jim Westphal from the University of Michigan examined an intriguing aspect of CEO behavior, and that is their inclination to seek advice from others.

CEOs often seek advice on strategic issues from executives of other firms. However, we also know from research that, just like the rest of us, they are often inclined to solicit that "advice" from friends and other people who are just like them. In such cases,

❝ People seek confirmation that what they are doing is right, and what better way to get that than by asking the opinion of your friends? ❞

it is not really genuine advice-seeking, but it serves more in a self-confirmatory fashion; people seek confirmation that what they are doing is right, and what better way to get that than by asking the opinion of your friends?

To examine which CEOs engage in this pseudo advice-seeking and which ones truly turn to people who might actually disagree with them, McDonald and his colleagues surveyed 225 large American industrial and service firms. They managed to obtain information on how often their CEOs sought the input of other top managers outside their own firm, and how well acquainted they were to them. Subsequently, they statistically correlated that to the extent to which these top managers received performance-contingent compensation packages, and found a very clear result.

Those CEOs who had a very small performance-related pay component in their compensation package sought very little true external advice. They relied on asking their friends – and perhaps their wife, uncles, and mother – whether they too thought that what they were doing was great, splendid, and spot on.

In contrast, CEOs with a relatively large performance-contingent component in their remuneration package sought advice much more often from other executives who were not their friends and who had different backgrounds than themselves. These people may be slightly scary (they might actually tell you that what you're saying is nonsense!) but perhaps also more useful. Moreover, McDonald and colleagues showed that this true advice-seeking significantly helped the financial performance of the CEOs' companies, in the form of an increase in the company's market-to-book and return on assets. Thus, the scary stuff actually led to hard cash!

The pay-for-performance construction paid off; it stimulated executives to repress their "it's-only-human" inclination to avoid asking the opinion of people who might actually disagree with you. It is much safer and less threatening to solicit advice from people who will say that you're splendid, but it is much more useful – and lucrative – to really put yourself to the test. And if you reward them for it, and only if you reward them for it, CEOs – like most people – will actually be brave enough to take this test.

Dirty laundry: who is hiding the bad stuff?

Let me end this chapter with a bit of intrigue. Are firms sometimes inclined to conceal negative information, for instance in their communications to shareholders? What do you think? Ah ... I guess I'm becoming predictable ...

Some years back, two researchers – Eric Abrahamson from Columbia Business School and Choelsoon Park, at the time at the London Business School – examined this question systematically. Their answer – perhaps not surprisingly – was "yes".

Fortunately, however, they did not stop there. Because perhaps a more interesting question is, "Who is concealing the bad stuff?" or, put differently, which firms are inclined to hide their dirty laundry?

Eric and Choelsoon investigated so-called letters to shareholders of 1,118 companies as published in these firms' annual reports. There is quite a bit of evidence that these letters to shareholders form one of the main communication devices of firms to their shareholders and that they have a real impact on companies' share price. Eric and Choelsoon, through computer analysis of the wording of these letters, measured how much negative information was disclosed in them.

In addition, they collected information on a bunch of other variables, such as the firms' (subsequent) performance, the percentage of outside directors on their boards, shares held by those outside directors, institutional ownership of the companies, auditor reports, etc. And they uncovered some pretty gritty stuff.

Their first finding was: company presidents – who officially write these letters – are tempted to lie and hide their company's bad news. I reckon that is only human. My guess is many of us might be tempted to tone down our failures (and play up our achieve-ments a bit) in such public statements, to not feel embarrassed and make ourselves look more successful. But there are things that can be done, in terms of corporate governance, to stem their and our natural inclination to obscure the truth.

That brings me to finding number two: Eric and Choelsoon showed that having outside directors on the board made firms lie less. The more outside directors firms had, the more forthcoming they were with their bad news. Similarly, having large institutional investors prompted firms to be more open about their failures in these letters to shareholders. Large institutional investors tended to monitor the firms they invest in quite closely, which apparently gave them less opportunity to conceal the negative stuff.

But then came finding number three: If we gave our outside directors shares in the company, the results flipped! Firms that had outside directors who also were major shareholders were *less* forthcoming in disclosing their bad news. It seems that having an ownership stake in the company created a conflict of interest for these people which induced them to stimulate their firm to hide its dirty laundry rather than disclose it.

Moreover, having lots of small institutional investors – who don't scrutinize companies as strictly – also made the results flip: firms with lots of small institutional investors hid their bad news more often, probably because they were afraid these investors would run at the slightest hint of bad news (which they are indeed known to do), which could snowball and send the firm's share price plummeting. To conclude, having outside directors may be a good thing, but only if they don't have a lot of shares. Institutional investors may be a good thing too, but only if they do have a big stake.

By the way, interestingly, Eric and Choelsoon also found that those companies that did not disclose their bad news were exactly the companies whose top managers would quickly sell a whole bunch of their privately held shares shortly after the release of the (over-optimistic) letter to shareholders. I guess corporate crooks don't only lie: they also steal.

6

Myths in management

No stranger to fiction

This chapter deals with management practices – stuff that companies do to make their organizations work better, which they often copy from others – and there are lots of them. Many of these practices, however, have unintended consequences. This chapter exposes the unexpected consequences of several of these practices. The good news is that these effects are not all bad! For example, did you know that an R&D department that never comes up with anything new can still be useful? Yes, it can.

On the other hand, some of these management practices ... how can I put it mildly ... well ... they don't do a fricking thing at all. Really, they don't work! And don't think that just because everybody's doing them, and telling you great stories about them, they are any good. Some of them are just plain useless – at best.

In this chapter, I will introduce you to a number of well-known management practices, which are widely used throughout the world of business, and then tell you what we actually know about their effects from scientific research. It requires the temporal suspension of disbelief, a good dose of management demystification, and the occasional bout of corporate exorcism. Hence, this chapter, like Chapter 5, relies heavily on hard research facts.

It details how practices (in spite of sometimes dubious effects) can still spread and become popular. Prepare to be exposed to bandwagons, self-fulfilling prophecies, and patent sharks.

Say you will – that'll do

I ended Chapter 5 with some exposures of top management remuneration. While the question of how to reward CEOs and other top executives is an ongoing area of discussion and research, one thing that pretty much everyone seems to agree on is that, of course, executive compensation should be closely tied to the performance of the firm.*

However, it is not easy to measure "the performance of the firm". Performance in terms of what? And performance over what period? Therefore, a decade or two ago, the use of so-called "long-term incentive plans" came about; simply put, top executives receive rewards (in the form of stock or cash) on specific dates dependent on whether specific performance goals are met. Such incentive plans are thought to much more precisely link rewards to managerial performance, encouraging executives to direct their attention to long-term profitability rather than short-term gains.

The stock market (that is, investors and analysts) loves them. Ample studies in financial economics show that when firms announce the adoption of long-term incentive plans (for example, through press releases or proxy statements), their stock price immediately shoots up. Managers may not always like them – getting rewarded (or not) based on very specific targets at very specific points in time can spoil the fun a bit – but it was also hard to resist them; not adopting one of those thingies made you look "illegitimate". Hence, the top managers of many firms decided to adopt them after all.

Professors James Westphal from the University of Michigan and Ed Zajac of Northwestern University decided to study the stock-market effects of these long-term incentive plans once again, but they did something more. First, as expected, examining 408 large US companies, they too found that adopting firms' share prices

---

* Although I have to admit that I might be an exception to this rule ...
I sometimes cannot suppress the thought that giving top managers a fixed salary might not be a superior solution.

went up immediately when they announced that they were going to install such an incentive plan.

Then Jim and Ed also examined whether it mattered how you worded the announcement statement. Specifically, they measured whether the firm's justification for adopting the incentive plan explained that it did so to tie CEO compensation more closely to shareholder wealth (that is, "all the right reasons" for investors; for instance, global aluminum producer Alcoa did this), instead of a more general description, for instance some sort of HR reason ("this plan enhances our ability to attract talent"; AT&T) or no explanation at all. And they found that upon announcement, the stock price of the firms "who used all the right words" went up by 2.4 percent, while the stock price of the other firms announcing the same plan (but using some other type of explanation) only increased by half of that (1.2 percent). That is, some firms gained benefits twice from the same thing, by only choosing their words a bit more carefully! That's easy money.

Then, though, it got really interesting. Next, Jim and Ed examined what happened to the stock price of the firms that announced that they were going to adopt a long-term incentive plan but, subsequently, did not actually do it … (a whopping 52 percent of firms did this!).

This is what they found: first, they found that the stock price of those firms went up on announcement of the plan just like it did for the others (and why not, the stock market could not yet know they were not actually going to implement it!). Then Jim and Ed measured what happened to the stock price the week following the announcement (when they still had not actually implemented the scheme). Nothing; the stock price was still up. Then they measured what had happened after a month; the stock price was still up … Then they measured the outcome after a full year; the stock price was still up…!

Stock prices went up after announcing the incentive plan. Stock prices did not go down even when the firm subsequently did not actually implement the scheme! Speak about easy money!!

Is the stock market stupid, or what? Well ... perhaps the answer is partly "yes" ... but it is probably also a bit more subtle than that. Apparently you and I, investors and analysts, care about firms using the right language, but we care much less about *what* they actually do. Hence, we reward their symbolic behavior, rather than their actual behavior. We may not even be fully aware of it, but that's what we value: unlike Caesar's wife Pompeia (who, according to Caesar, not only had to be virtuous but also appear virtuous), we want a firm to appear virtuous, yet we don't care whether it really is!

Right again! Managers and their self-fulfilling prophecies

I realize that, by now, over the past chapters, I must have been giving you the impression that I am slightly skeptical about the mental abilities of people in business, including top managers. But that's a faulty impression, honest! Well, that is ... I do actually think they have only limited mental abilities ... But what I am mostly trying to point out is that that is because they are only human. Or, let's say, near human (just like business-school professors and other suspected mutations of the human genome) because they do suffer an awful lot from self-fulfilling prophecies. Let me give you an example.

My former colleague at the London Business School, Olay Sorenson (now at the University of Toronto), together with his colleague David Waguespack, examined distributors in the US movie industry. Distributors have certain preconceived ideas about what movies will be a success at the box office – for instance, the number of stars in the movie, the actors' prior successes, previous experience of the production team, etc.

When Sorenson and Waguespack analyzed data on over 5,000 movies, they discovered that these distributors seemed correct in their beliefs; movies that corresponded to their prior beliefs indeed reaped higher revenue at the box office.

Then Sorenson and Waguespack did a clever thing; they also analyzed the scarce resources that these distributors assigned to their movies, such as budget, promotion efforts, number of screens on opening day, favorable timing in the year (e.g., around Christmas many more people go to the cinema). What they found was striking: the reason why those movies that the executives had high hopes for beforehand indeed did become successes could 100 percent be explained by the fact that the distributors, in their subsequent allocation of resources, significantly favored them.

When Sorenson and Waguespack, in their statistical analysis, corrected for the fact that distributors assigned so much of their scarce resources to those movies, it turned out that the executives' assessments were completely wrong; those movies usually did comparatively worse at the box office! The only reason why the movies that they had first thought would become successes indeed did reap "profits" is because they assigned more resources to them. Yet, they would have been better off assigning the scarce resources to the other movies. The executives' prior beliefs were false; they just seemed correct afterwards due to their own, self-confirming actions.

❝ Human beings develop prior beliefs about what will work and what won't ❞

Do such self-fulfilling prophecies only exist in Hollywood? My guess is not. Self-confirming dynamics abound everywhere. Human beings develop prior beliefs about what will work and what won't, and subsequently (unconsciously) work hard to make sure they're right. And, after all, top managers are only human too.

Your expectations manage you

Self-fulfilling prophecies can be found in various forms in the religious tales and texts in many cultures (e.g., Greek, Indian, Arabic). They also often feature in fairy tales (Enron comes to mind) and psychology studies. For example, when teachers are led to believe that a particular student has great potential, the student often will begin to outperform his peers. This is simply because extra attention from the teacher, the student's subsequent surge in self-confidence, positive feedback from the initial results, and so forth, actually make the (in reality ordinary) student perform better. The famous sociologist Robert Merton first labeled this effect a "self-fulfilling prophecy".

And the world of business – and the economy in general – is rife with them. Let me give you another example. It concerns a study that was conducted in the 1970s by Professor Albert King, at the time a professor of management and industrial relations at Kansas State University (also summarized aptly in *The Production of Knowledge* by Bill Starbuck).

Albert conducted an experiment in four different plants owned by the same company. The managers of plants 1 and 2 were told, by the company's director of manufacturing, to experiment with "job enlargement" practices, in which machine crews had to both set up their machines and inspect their own finished work. The other two plants, 3 and 4, were asked to implement "job rotation" practices, in which workers switched tasks at scheduled intervals. Thus, Albert's experiment appeared to be comparing the results of job enlargement with those of job rotation.

Then Albert did a cunning thing: he lied. Because he introduced one other crucial difference between the plants. The managers of plants 1 and 3 were told that past research implied that the job changes would raise productivity, while the managers of plants 2 and 4 were led to believe that past research implied that the job changes would improve "industrial relations" (which should result in lower absenteeism).

Subsequently, for a period of 12 months, Albert measured both productivity and absenteeism levels at the four plants. Analyzing the data, it turned out that where the plant managers had been told to expect higher productivity, productivity became 6 percent higher; where the plant managers had been told to expect better industrial relations, absenteeism was 12 percent lower, regardless of whether they implemented job-enlargement or job-rotation practices!

The changes in workers' actual activities really had no influence; productivity at the two job-enlargement plants hardly differed at all, nor did absenteeism at the two job-rotation plants. The plant managers' expectations caused all the effects.

Albert wrote, "the results provide evidence that managerial expectations concerning performance may serve as a self-fulfilling prophecy". People somehow achieve what they (are led to) believe will happen, regardless of any actual changes made to the organization. This is where management (and the science of management) departs from the hard sciences: predictions of the return of Halley's comet do not influence its orbit, but being told whether we're stars or crap at our jobs influences our subsequent achievements.

> **66 but being told whether we're stars or crap at our jobs influences our subsequent achievements 99**

"Reverse causality" – sorry, but life's not that simple

Let me also introduce you to a related phenomenon called "reverse causality". Have you ever heard of or even read some of these best-selling business books: *In Search of Excellence, Built to Last,* or *Profit from the Core*? Their authors usually follow a simple, yet appealing, formula. They look at a number of very successful companies, see what they have in common, then conclude "this must be a good thing!", write a book recommending everybody should do the same thing, and become millionaires. Yet, reality – and management research – is really a bit trickier than that …

One conclusion many of these business books draw is that one should focus on a limited set of "core activities". For example, as Professor Jerker Denrell from the University of Oxford showed, *Profit from the Core* authors Chris Zook and James Allan find that 78 percent of the high-performing firms in their sample of 1,854 companies focus on just one set of core activities, while a mere 22 percent of the low-performing companies did. Hence, they conclude that companies should focus. Simple isn't it? Yeah, but a bit too simple …

What this "advice" ignores is that often underperforming companies diversify into other businesses in order to try to find more rewarding markets. Thus, their "non-focus" is the *result* of poor performance, rather than the cause! In contrast, it's very common for very successful companies to narrow their strategic focus in order to concentrate on the business that brings them most success. Again, their focus is not the cause of their success; it is the result of it. Our best-selling business-book friends are reversing cause and effect; recommending everybody to apply more focus may be dubious advice at best!

Similarly, many of these business books conclude that the high-performing companies they looked at all had very strong and homogeneous corporate cultures. Hence, they conclude: create a strong corporate culture! Seductively simple again … Unfortunately, not so sound.

It is a well-known effect in academic research that success may gradually start to *create* a homogeneous organizational culture. Again, the coherent culture is not the *cause* of the company's success, but the result of it! What's worse, a narrow, dogmatic corporate culture may lead to trouble. When the firm's business environment changes – and business environments eventually do – it makes the company rigid and unable to adapt: the phenomenon I discussed in Chapter 2, known as the success trap.

Indeed, the authors of *In Search of Excellence*, (1982) Peters and Waterman, who analyzed 43 of "the most excellent companies in the world", also concluded that a strong corporate culture was a necessity for business stardom. However, if you look at their list of 43 "most excellent companies" today, only three or four might still make the list (Johnson & Johnson, Intel, Wal-Mart, Mars); the remainder has fallen off the list or disappeared altogether.

Hence, remember that "association is not causation". For example, that successful companies are associated with a very focused set of business activities and strong corporate cultures does not mean that this is what caused their success. Importantly, trying to replicate these symptoms of success may actually prevent you from attaining it.

Eating Uncle Ed – don't worry, it's called downsizing

Allow me to tell you another story in a similar vein (although perhaps you may want to skip this bit if you tend to visualize what you read). About a century ago, the Fore people, who inhabited Papua New Guinea, had the habit of burying their deceased relatives, just like many other societies. Yet, one sunny day, Uncle Ed died, at around lunch-time. Uncle Ed's relatives were about to put him into the ground when one of his cousins (who looked particularly hungry) said, "Why bury all that good meat? It's a waste; we might as well eat it." And so they did.

When, the following month, another relative died, they did the same thing, and soon, the whole village was eating their deceased relatives, rather than putting them into the ground. The advantages were obvious; there had actually been quite a bit of famine and malnutrition among the Fore people and this habit enabled them simply to not be so hungry.

Some time later, a visitor from a neighboring village witnessed the practice. When he got home and his cousin died, he quickly convinced his relatives to, rather than bury the good chap, consume him on the spot. Gradually the practice started spreading to all villages in the tribe, until the habit of eating deceased relatives had become the norm and the Fore's proud tradition.

Yet, unfortunately, they ate everything, including their relatives' brains. As a consequence, they developed a horrible, lethal disease called Kuru (which is related to Creutzfeld–Jacob, a.k.a. mad cow disease). The disease has quite a long incubation time (i.e., it takes several years before it becomes apparent) but eventually the Fore people started getting sick and dying en masse. Of course, they noticed something was seriously wrong but, due to the disease's long incubation time, had no idea that their misery was caused by the habit of eating their deceased. The practice continued until half of the Fore population had been wiped out and Australian invaders put an end to it (because they thought it was gross, not because they understood it caused the disease).

Why am I telling you this story – after all, you might be reading this just before lunch? The reason is as follows: many managers and companies remind me of the Fore people. Let me explain: the Fore's practice clearly was detrimental; after all, it was killing them! Yet, the reason for them adopting it was clear too: the practice gave them an immediate advantage, namely less hunger and less starvation. In the long run, however, they were definitely worse off for doing it, but the problem was that, due to the practice's incubation time, they could not understand it was this habit they had picked up many years ago that was causing the problems.

Quite a few popular management practices have the same characteristics. The problems they cause only occur in the long run and are therefore underestimated or not understood at all, but the benefits are immediate.

Take, for example, the practice of "downsizing" (or rationalizing, restructuring, reorganizing, etc.: that is, making people redundant). It is a trend that has now been going on for at least a decade and a half; companies – even if they are not in financial difficulties – engage in systematic programs to reduce the headcount in their organizations. The short-term benefits are clear: it leads to lower costs (sometimes accompanied by a positive response from the stock market to the announcement of the program). Yet, there is also evidence of sizeable long-term detrimental influences, such as reduced innovation and lower employee commitment and loyalty. However, such consequences are only noticeable in the long run.

Usually, when a firm faces a serious problem, for example due to a lack of new products in the pipeline, top management does not realize that the lack of innovation is caused by the downsizing program they engaged in a decade ago. Just as it did for the Fore people and their illness, the long lead-time makes it all but impossible for managers to connect and understand cause and effect. Thus, not only will top management take inappropriate action to solve the problem (often another cost-cutting program …), but it also remains unclear to other firms that downsizing is harmful, leading them to adopt and continue the practice too.

Cause and effect are often a tricky thing in the world of business. When a certain management practice gives us immediate benefits, we are inclined to assume it must be a good one. However, the presence of short-term benefits does not mean that the overall, long-term consequences are all that healthy! Yet, when they finally materialize, we don't quite grasp that the practice has caused them. In the world of business, it is often hard to gain an understanding of the long-term consequences of our decisions. Yet, you do want to make sure you really think through the consequences, because before you know it, you have eaten Uncle Ed.

“ Cause and effect are often a tricky thing in the world of business. „

Does downsizing ever work?

So, let's think a bit more about the practice of downsizing. What is the evidence for its effects? Does it actually work ... like, ever? Let me give you a sneak preview in a nutshell: no, it doesn't.

Workforce downsizing has been a popular pastime lately (i.e., over the past decade or two), with more and more companies announcing mass lay-off programs, even if they're not in financial trouble. The practice started in the early 1980s, when economic slowdown more or less forced firms into it, but proved not to be a passing trend when in the ensuing decades many firms continued to engage in systematic workforce reductions.

Of course, firms engage in downsizing hoping to boost their profitability. But does it work? It has obvious advantages – waving the hatchet tends to lower headcount quite effectively, which obviously leaves you with lower labour expenses – but also has some potential disadvantages, such as lower commitment and loyalty among the survivors. It is not immediately clear whether the positives will outweigh the negatives, or vice versa.

66 firms engage in downsizing hoping to boost their profitability 99

Therefore, Professors James Guthrie, from the University of Kansas, and Deepak Datta, from the University of Texas at Arlington, decided to research the issue in a systematic way. They managed to obtain in-depth data on 122 firms that had engaged in downsizing, and performed various statistical techniques to examine whether the program had improved their profitability. The answer was "no".

Beforehand, James and Deepak had thought that downsizing would likely be harmful for firms that rely heavily on people (such as firms in industries in which R&D is very important, or firms with low capital intensity) and firms that are in growth industries (since it would be more difficult to justify mass lay-offs there). And they were right; in those type of businesses, downsizing programs significantly reduced firms' subsequent profitability.

However, they had also expected the reverse to be true; that firms in industries in which people were less central to companies' competitive advantage (firms in industries with low R&D, firms with high capital intensity) and firms in low-growth industries would be able to get away with downsizing programs, and increase their profitability as a result. Yet, they proved to be wrong. Even in such businesses, downsizing didn't help a single bit, and usually lowered performance. In fact, they couldn't find a single business in which downsizing proved beneficial for firms.

To conclude, the average company did not benefit from a downsizing effort, no matter what situation and industry they were in. Of course, firms in trouble need to do something. However, simply reducing your headcount won't do the trick.

Who can downsize without detriment?

Why do downsizing programs not usually work? Well, for starters, as you can imagine, it is not a great motivator for the survivors. Academic studies confirm that organizational commitment usually decreases after a downsizing program and, for example, voluntary turnover rates surge. Hence, downsizing is not something to be taken lightly, and should be avoided if at all possible. But sometimes, of course, a company's situation may have become so dire that it may not be avoidable. What then? Who might be able to get away with it?

Professors Charlie Trevor and Anthony Nyberg from the University of Wisconsin-Madison decided to examine this question, surveying several hundreds of companies in the US on their downsizing efforts, voluntary turnover rates, and HR practices. As expected, they too found that for most companies, voluntary turnover rates increased significantly after a downsizing program. Many of the survivors, earmarked to guide the company through its process of recovery, decided to call it a day after all and continue their employment somewhere else – an unexpected aftershock for many slimmed-down companies; they became quite a bit leaner than intended!

Next, however, Professors Trevor and Nyberg examined who could get away with a downsizing program or, put differently, what sort of companies did not suffer from such an unexpected surge in voluntary turnover after their downsizing program. And the answer was pretty clear. Companies that had a history of harboring HR practices that were aimed at ensuring procedural fairness and justice – such as having an ombudsman to address employee complaints, confidential hotlines for problem resolution, the existence of grievance or appeal processes for non-union employees, etc. – did not see their turnover increase after a downsizing effort. Apparently, remaining employees were confident that, in such a company, the downsizing effort had been fair and unavoidable.

Similarly, Trevor and Nyberg found that companies with paid sabbaticals, on-site childcare, defined benefit plans, and flexible or non-standard arrival and departure times did much better in limiting the detrimental effects of a downsizing program. The surviving employees were more understanding of the company's efforts, had higher commitment, or simply found the firm too good a place to desert!

In general, it shows downsizing can work, but only if you have always taken commitment to your people seriously. Instead, if your employees sense that you may be taking the issue lightly, they will vote with their feet. And you may end up losing rather more people than you had bargained for. Or as *Fortune* magazine once observed, most firms that downsize, "rather than becoming lean and mean, often end up lean and lame".

❝ downsizing can work, but only if you have always taken commitment to your people seriously ❞

What management bandwagons bring

Let's consider some other (slightly dubious) management practices: management by objectives, zero-based budgeting, T groups, theory Y, theory Z, diversification, matrix organization, participative management, management by walking around, job enlargement, quality circles, re-engineering, total quality management, teams, Six Sigma, ISO 9000, and empowerment for starters.

Surely you must have been subjected to some of those? Most of them have fallen out of favor again. We call them management fads. But do they do anything? Well ... the answer is "yes", but perhaps not what you'd expect them to do, or what they are intended to do.

Professors Barry Staw and Lisa Epstein, both from University of California in Berkeley, through careful statistical analysis, examined some of the consequences of organizations adopting such techniques on a variety of factors. They collected data on exactly 100 Fortune 500 companies, including their adoption of quality techniques (such as total quality management), teams and empowerment, the company's reputation (through *Fortune's* "Most Admired Companies" survey), their financial performance and, of course, CEOs' compensation. This is what they found.

Firms adopting popular management techniques (such as TQM, etc.) did subsequently not perform any better than firms not adopting them. Actually, if Barry and Lisa did find an effect of any of the techniques, it was negative. Usually, though, the stuff didn't have any effect at all.

Then they examined the effect of adopting such techniques on the companies' reputation, measured through their position and ascent on *Fortune* magazine's "Most Admired Companies" list. The analysis revealed clearly that adoption of the popular management techniques significantly increased firms' position on the "Most Admired Companies" list, irrespective of their performance. To be precise, those firms were rated as being more innovative and as having higher quality management. Apparently, the stuff doesn't actually have to work for it to enhance your reputation in the outside world.

Finally the pièce de résistance: the influence of the adoption of popular management techniques on a CEO's compensation package (salary and bonus) ... Yep, you guessed it, and the effects were very strong: if a CEO's firm adopted one of the popular management techniques, his compensation went up.

So what does this tell us? Well, first of all of course that many of these management fads simply don't work. The organization doesn't perform better as a result of adopting any of them. Yet, apparently, it does make you look innovative and legitimate in the eyes of others. This includes fellow executives, who subsequently vote for you as being "much admired" but – hurrah! – also in the eyes of your board; they enthusiastically pat you on the back for the great achievement and, with grace and thanks, increase the size of your compensation package.

Remember this one: "total quality management"?

Many popular management practices, as scientific research persistently shows, are quite useless. They simply don't work. Yet, they're often imitated. As discussed in previous chapters, that's largely because firms have a general inclination to imitate each other, and that certainly includes imitating silly things.

Mark Zbaracki, a professor at Wharton, found himself examining total quality management (TQM) techniques in the early 1990s, when the thing was at its heyday. He made extensive visits to five organizations – a defense contractor, a hotel, a hospital, a manufacturing firm and a government agency – to figure out how they came about adopting TQM.

A very consistent pattern emerged. Invariably, when management started to hear about this "new thing" called total quality management, they signed up for seminars and conferences in which representatives from other firms spoke about their experiences of the implementation of TQM. There they would hear about the substantial improvements TQM had brought them, often larded with impressive statistics and commanding jargon. It didn't take long and the managers became convinced that they too had to adopt this new technique, or risk falling behind forever.

So they started sending their people to TQM training courses and hired consultants that specialized in the new techniques, through which they learned more stories about the power of TQM and its remarkable results. Soon, they put their considerable weight behind a pilot: one department would experiment with the new techniques, so that others could learn from them.

This was often followed by the introduction of a series of internal seminars, a quarterly TQM newsletter sent to all departments within the organization, and the appointment of dedicated internal TQM experts. Subsequently, all these parties were told to publicize the firm's early "success stories" to enthral others and raise enthusiasm in the rest of the company to embrace the new technique.

Soon, the newsletters found their way to people at other companies, and the organization's managers started to receive invites to come and share their success stories at TQM conferences and seminars. Yet, in reality, for every "success story" there were always a handful of failures. Yet, those stories did not find their way into the newsletters, the company's external communications, or the manager's slick seminar slide pack.

And in the conference room, the attending managers who had heard about this new technique were in awe of the substantial improvements that TQM had brought the speaker's firm, and they were impressed with the optimistic statistics and commanding jargon. And they too went back to their firms, and proclaimed that they really had to adopt this new technique, or risk falling behind forever.

The spread of the management practice becomes a self-enforcing cycle. It almost acts like the rabies virus. As Professor Richard Dawkins explained in *The Selfish Gene*, the virus's well-known hydrophobic symptom, causing an infected dog's mouth to "foam", encourages it to shake the wet from its mouth and with it the virus. This promotes the virus's spread. Moreover, it turns a dog into a restless wanderer, propagating the virus even further afield.

Similarly, a silly management practice may be stimulated to increase in frequency if it comes with a mechanism that causes it to spread. So next time you are attending a business seminar, and the presenter tries to convince you with a flashy PowerPoint presentation of the brilliance of this new management technique they've been using, and you're feeling that you are about to be convinced, just imagine him as a dog with a foaming mouth, and then think again.

ISO 9000 makes you reliable, myopic, efficient, and dull – and unable to invent Post-It notes

Sometimes, management practices, intended to improve the functioning of an organization, are not merely ineffective but have unanticipated consequences. Sometimes these consequences are negative but only apparent in the long run, making firms adopt techniques which are really not very healthy for them (at least in the long run).

Take ISO 9000. ISO 9000 certification constitutes a process management technique through which firms are expected to follow (and document) a number of procedures, aimed at creating consistent, efficient processes, in which best practices are standardized and deviations from the best practice are avoided. It leads to efficient, high-quality products with minimal digression from the standard.

This all sounds very logical, justified and desirable, right? So what am I whining about?

Well, Professors Mary Benner from the University of Pennsylvania and Mike Tushman from the Harvard Business School examined what happened to the innovation output of firms adopting ISO 9000 techniques. They collected information on 98 firms in the photography industry and 17 firms in the paint industry, which they followed from 1980 till 1999. They measured, among others, all their patents and documented whether these innovations were really "close to home" for the firm (representing minor variations on what they were already doing) or more exploratory discoveries (representing truly new potential avenues for growth). And they found a very clear pattern.

Firms that adopted ISO 9000 norms started doing significantly more "close to home" inventions at the expense of truly new, exploratory innovation. The "more of the same" patents, induced by the ISO 9000 processes, crowded out the discovery of truly new techniques and products.

How come? Well, by definition, ISO 9000 minimizes deviations from "the best way of doing things" in the firm. Yet, often, the best innovations are discovered by accident. Just like random genetic mutations can produce whole new species in nature, random deviations from the norm in organizations sometimes turn out to be "mistakes" which become the firm's next big blockbuster product. Think of how the Post-It note came into existence: a bloke named Spencer Silver was working in the 3M research laboratories in 1970 trying to find a super-strong adhesive. Spencer developed a new adhesive, but it was ridiculously weak. It was so weak that although it stuck to objects, it could easily be lifted off. It was a clear error. Yet, ultimately, this super-weak adhesive became 3M's famous, money-spinning Post-It note.

Although usually deviations from the norm merely produce mistakes, which should get corrected quickly, if you rule out all mistakes, you will never be fortunate enough to develop a "mistake" that turns out to be your Post-It note. ISO 9000 annuls all deviations from the norm. But, as a result (unintended), you become a lousy inventor.

How bad practice prevails

When speaking to executives, I always make a point of quizzing them about their management practices. Quite often, when I interview or just talk to a manager about his company and try to figure out why it is organized or managed in a particular way, I hit upon something which I don't understand: some practice, management technique, service specification or incentive system which I fail to grasp why they do it like that (just to name a few candidates: detailing in pharmaceuticals, buy-back guarantees in book publishing, insane working hours in investment banking). And when I ask, "I am not sure I understand; can you explain a bit more?", I often get a long and waffly answer (which suggests to me that they don't quite know why either ...).

And when I then, stubbornly, poke a bit harder ("Sorry, but I still don't get it ..."), the interviewee might get annoyed, and then I will receive the momentous reply "Look, Freek, everybody in our business does it this way, and everybody has always been doing it like this; if this wasn't the best way to do things, I am sure it would have disappeared by now."

I never quite bought this answer but, frankly, did not quite know how to refute it.

Because our well-established theories of economic organization would propagate exactly that: the market is Darwinian. Firms with bad habits and practices have a lower chance of making it in the market in comparison to smart firms that do everything right. Therefore, those firms will go out of business quicker and, although it may take a while, the ineffective practices will die out with them.

But I still thought they were wrong. I now think I have figured it out. Bad practices can spread and persist in industries. Let me attempt to explain to you how and why.

The trick is bad management practices can survive, despite making firms worse off, just like viruses can persist among humans. Because they are contagious, and spread quicker than they kill, the virus (or management practice) can continue to persist and not die out.

Moreover, what's unique about industries is that if everybody is employing the practice, everybody is equally bad. Yet, because competition is based on relative competitive strength, firms might not even notice that they are worse off for continuing the silly habit. Customers might complain about them (e.g., "all the high-street banks are equally terrible!") but don't have a choice; they have to pick one anyway (just as they would if the banks were all excellent). Hence, the banks don't suffer.

> **❝ Many management practices act like viruses, spreading from one firm to the next, in spite of harmful consequences. ❞**

Many of these management practices (like TQM and ISO 9000) do act like viruses, spreading from one firm to the next, in spite of harmful consequences. This also implies that, just like a virus, the practice continues to exist. It may seem paradoxical but it is possible that, although a particular management practice lowers firms' effectiveness, and everybody would be better off without it, it persists over time.

You can put these things into simulation – which I did, just to show that it works – and quite easily model the diffusion and persistence of harmful management practices. So, next time a manager tells you they do it because everybody has always done it and they're sure that therefore it must be the best way of doing things, just smile at him and say "Ah! That's not necessarily true; just because everybody is doing it and has been doing it like this forever, does not mean that it is the best way of doing things."

DAVE Carpenter

"IMPLEMENTING THESE CHANGES WON'T BE EASY.
WE'RE PRETTY SET IN DOING THINGS THE WRONG WAY."

Can we please stop saying that the market is efficient?

Actually, the idea that management practices act like viruses has potential implications for how we view the workings of our whole economy, and the efficiency of the market on which most countries in the world base their economic model.

The famous economist Jovanovic wrote, about a quarter of a century ago, "efficient firms grow and survive; inefficient firms decline and fail". What he meant is that the market is Darwinian; it will rule out the least efficient firms, with habits and practices that make them perform comparatively badly, and it will make sure efficient firms prosper, so that only good business practices prevail.

Yeah, right.

When you look around you, in the world of business, one sometimes can't help wonder where Darwin went wrong ... How come we see so many firms that drive us up the wall, how come we see silly business practices persisting (excessive risk-taking, dubious governance mechanisms, corporate sexism, grey suits and ties, to name an eclectic few), and how come so many – sometimes well-educated and intelligent – people continue to have an almost unshakable belief that the market really is efficient, and that it will make the best firms prevail if you just give it time?

That's because the logic is not entirely wrong. The market is Darwinian, and the firms with the highest level of "fitness" are the ones most likely to prevail. However, our Darwinian view of business is also so simplistic that I am unsure whether it would make Mister Charles Robert Darwin cringe, burst out laughing, or pull the hairs from his bulging beard in agony. Darwinian mechanisms – or market mechanisms if you prefer – work at different levels. And sometimes they conflict. Let me explain.

Some business practices, like the ones mentioned above, will actually reduce the fitness levels of the firms that adopt them, and make them less efficient, yet they persist. That's because these practices have a fitness level of their own. The flu kills many thousands of people every year, and at first glance it seems a slightly flawed strategy of the virus to kill one's host, yet it persists. Why is that? That's because it spreads quicker than it kills. It doesn't matter much, for a virus, that it reduces the fitness of its host, as long as it jumps to someone else before the host snuffs it! And in a way that is what bad business practices do too. They spread easily, and kill slowly and stealthily.

Firms don't know that the practice is bad. Very bad practices are easy to spot, so nobody adopts them, but not these ones! They're sneaky – you catch it before you realize it, and the negative effects only become apparent in the long run, just like the eating habits of the Fore people.

An example, you say? Well, I explained earlier how downsizing takes its toll, yet remains popular. Similarly, a few pages ago I discussed scientific findings on the consequences of adopting ISO 9000, especially when applied in a very innovative industry. The research I discussed – by Professors Benner from the University of Pennsylvania and Tushman from the Harvard Business School – showed that ISO 9000, in the long run, can have a severe negative impact on a firm because it hampers innovation. Yet, the short-term benefits are clear; adopting ISO 9000 often comes with some good reputational effects, an immediate increase in customers, and satisfied stakeholders. However, the negative effect on innovation, in the long run, may outweigh all of this.

Nevertheless, firms adopt practices because they see the short-term benefits, but are quite unaware of the long-run detrimental stuff. To managers in charge of improving their firms' performance now, the practice seems attractive because they noticed that companies in other industries (perhaps not so reliant on innovation) benefited greatly at the time they adopted it, many of the firm's competitors are currently adopting it, and they all see a surge in customer applications too! Of course it looks attractive!

Moreover, once we start to suffer from a shortage of internal innovation, many years will have passed, and no-one quite realizes that the creeping troubles were originally triggered by the adoption of the ISO 9000 practice a long time ago. The practice is adopted by many firms and continues to persist, despite the fact that everybody would be better off without it.

The same may very well be true for quite a few of our popular governance mechanisms, the practice of excessive risk-taking, as we saw it, in investment banking, many forms of performance management systems, and certainly for corporate sexism, and pin-striped suits with purple ties on a hot summer afternoon. It is not that Darwin is wrong – and the mechanisms he discovered do not rule our markets – it is just that they're just as difficult to shake off as a common cold. And they are just as annoying.

Pin-striped pigeons

Management practices, just like viruses, spread by hopping from one firm to the next. But often, just like viruses, they get a bit of third-party help. In the case of management practices, that third party is often a consultant. And that is because management consultants are a bit like rats. Or, to put it more kindly, pigeons (referred to by the former London mayor Ken Livingstone as "rats with wings"). They spread diseases.

I have been working for a while on a large research project which analyzes the spread of harmful management practices (a dodgy type of control system, faulty financial instrument, counter-productive management technique, etc.). As previously discussed, one could conjecture that harmful management practices never see the light of day (wrong) or that if they accidentally do, they will always quickly die out and disappear (wrong again). But let me now focus on *how* these harmful practices actually spread across firms.

Yep, that's where the pin-striped pigeons come in – OK, some of them are rats. Because harmful management practices spread like a virus, the pattern of how they spread among firms can be modeled successfully using techniques from social anthro-pology on the diffusion of harmful cultural practices (such as foot-binding in China, female circumcision, etc.), which not coincidentally have been adopted from epidemiology.

As I have said before, a virus – like the flu – survives by spreading to a new host, preferably before the old one dies. Often, there are some creatures (e.g., rats) that facilitate the spread among the creatures of another species (e.g., humans). That's much of what management consultants do, even knowingly: picking up practices in one industry or country and recommending and applying them in others. Just like viruses or bacteria, some of these practices are not very helpful, to say the least (although, as explained, the harmful effects may only manifest themselves in the long run); others may have been useful in the original setting (e.g., industry) but completely inappropriate in the new one.

TQM, ISO 9000, six sigma and so on, all come with a herd of specialist consultants that help you implement it, and get infected too. Unintentionally – again, just like the poor pigeons in London's Trafalgar Square – management consultants promote the spread and persistence of the harmful practice. According to former Mayor Livingstone, they're best banned and starved to death.

Management consultants – happy slapping

Now, before I move on, let me also say something in defense of the management consultant, because it appears that it has gradually become one of those professions which are socially acceptable to mock. It seems it has been getting increasingly fashionable to openly dislike management consultants (but hire them anyway)! Now, I wouldn't say it is an entirely new fashion, but the loathing of the pin-striped mercenaries seems to be reaching new and unprecedented heights of late.

A short while ago, I was talking to three members of the top team of a British company (which will remain blissfully anonymous) who showed me the three main conclusions of their team's recent "strategy retreat" and, believe it or not, one of the three was "no more consultants!"

Now, what have these poor people done to deserve such a bad reputation anyway, eh?! Well …

It is an unprotected profession and every idiot can call himself a management consultant (and many do – I guess the remainder become professors). Yet, the reputable firms also seem to provoke their fair share of grunting, ground-spitting, and a wide array of hand gestures. Is it pure envy? Surely there must be some of that; seeing them walking hand-in-hand with the CEO on the way to an expensive restaurant for a PowerPoint presentation between the fifth and sixth course while overtly charging a couple thousand bucks might do that to you.

Yet, there must be something more. Perhaps it is the fact that the accountability of the consultant is nil; it is not that we withhold payment till the effects of the recommended strategy have become apparent in ten years' time (even if that was measurable).

Perhaps it is because everything they recommend has such a high value of déjà vu – "Didn't I say that at our last away-day?"

Or perhaps it is because management consultants en masse recommended corporate diversification in the 1970s, a refocus on core activities in the 1990s, told "old economy" firms to keep their "new economy" activities as strictly separate entities during the dot-com bubble but lately advised them to carefully integrate clicks and bricks, urged IT firms to get into consulting while currently stealthily de-merging them, etc.?

Who knows, but let's not pretend we knew better. Surely you have both bad and good consultants, just as you have bad and good clients. Some (if not many …) executives seem to use consultants, expecting them to say what they wanted to hear anyway.

Consultants are undoubtedly more useful if you are genuinely open to hear what they have to say about your strategy.

Consultants are undoubtedly more useful if you are genuinely open to hear what they have to say about your strategy. For example, scientific research has suggested that bringing in an outsider's view can seriously improve the quality of decision-making (however, often at the price of slowing it down). Yet, hiring a consultant is of course no reason to stop thinking for yourself. As Richard Dawkins said, "It is good to be open-minded, but not so open that your brain falls out."

Star knowledge workers – you really should not pay them that much, you know

Talking about brains, why do we pay certain employees so much? "Duh, because they make us a heck of a lot of money!" you might say. Sure, that may be true, but I guess that's not enough. When a team of five salespeople earns you $7 million, you might pay them $100,000 each. But when a team of five consultants, attorneys, or security analysts makes you $7 million, you often end up paying them $1 million each! And why do we do that?!

Perhaps because their skills are more specialized and scarce and if they walk out of the door we'd have a hard time replacing them? Sure, that may be true, but I guess that's not enough either. Because if we had a highly specialized sales team, with technical knowledge perfectly attuned to our particular product range, we would likely still not pay them $1 million each, although we'd have a hard time replacing them if they left. And that's because they too would not find it easy to find a replacement job. Their skills are so specialized, attuned to our particular product, that they would not be able to make the same kind of money for any other company, and hence would be much less valuable anywhere else, to anyone else. Nope, we don't have to pay them that much to keep them; they don't have anywhere else to go!

But the consultants, attorneys, and security analysts do. They can just take their Rolodex, their files, their client base and expertise with them, and stroll into the office and payroll of our competitor, and earn them the same $7 million, right?

Well … maybe not. We often think they can just "take it with them"; they think that they can just take it with them, and our competitor usually thinks they can just take it with them. But often we're all wrong.

For example, Professor Boris Groysberg, at the Harvard Business School, examined the portability of star security analysts' performance. Security analysts, as you may know, are employed by investment banks to analyze companies in a particular industry. They, among others, produce earnings forecasts, buy and sell recommendations, and detailed reports on individual companies. If they're any good – because they, for instance, produce quite accurate earnings forecasts – they can easily take home several million in salary and bonuses per year. Yes really.

Investment banks pay them so much because they think they can easily take their skills, financial models, industry contacts, etc. to a different bank if they wanted to, and analyze the same sectors and companies. However, Boris found that that is actually not as simple as it seems ...

He analyzed the performance of 316 top-ranked security analysts who switched firms, using rankings published by the Institutional Investor All-America Research Team poll. He found that star analysts who switched employers immediately experienced a significant decline in their performance. The effect was substantial. For example, the chance that a particular analyst would come out top of his sector's league table (having made the most accurate forecasts, etc.) would drop by 50 percent if he had just switched firms. Actually, on average, it would take such an analyst five years to recover and make up for the switch and subsequent drop in performance.

Hence, even security analysts, whose work seems highly individual and not at all dependent on the particular organization that they work for, experience a very significant decline in their performance when they switch firms. Apparently, the soft stuff, such as the intellectual capital imbedded in the fabric of the organization, their relationships with colleagues, and all sorts of other social and tacit processes (which are difficult to identify, observe, or even name!) play a huge role, even in the work of such star performers. Take them out of their

> **we probably all overestimate the portability of our star workers, and of ourselves ...**

organization and their ability vanishes with the severance of the social ties.

This means that we probably all overestimate the portability of our star workers, and of ourselves. ...

It also means we pay them too much.

Patent sharks

Another way in which companies try to protect and hold on to their exclusive knowledge is through patents. And that is where the patent sharks come in. You never heard of patent sharks?! You're kidding, right? OK, I'll admit it, I had never heard of them either. But they sound pretty scary, right? Well ... OK, perhaps not; the word "patent" sort of seems to take the edge out of the word "shark" a bit. Yet, now that I have learned more about them, I have to admit, I am starting to believe that they should send some shivers down your corporate spine; they really are quite creepy.

My colleague at the London Business School, Markus Reitzig, has been studying patent sharks at length. I always found IP (intellectual property) a bit of a bore when it comes to research topics but, admittedly, his research did remind me of *Jaws III*, but with briefcase, pin-striped suit and, importantly, a mob of solicitors to accompany him. Let me explain.

As you may know, when it comes to the effectiveness of patents, pharmaceuticals are an exception. In most industries, patents provide only very limited protection against imitation by competitors. Usually, the part of the product that is patent-"protected" can be substituted or "invented around". Therefore, what firms have started doing is to protect their products with as many patents as possible. So, it is not uncommon in some high-tech industries to have over 1,000 different patents to protect many little components in a firm's product. They figure, one of them may not do the trick but if you have a whole bunch of them, collectively they should give some protection.

Yet, since competitors do the same, as a result, researchers have long noticed that patents have become sort of a corporate currency. How does this work? Well, whatever you want to do, in terms of developing a new product or technology, you're bound to infringe on someone's patent. Luckily, that someone is likely to need to infringe on some of your patents too. Rather than going to court, firms usually strike a deal: "I will forgive you for infringing on these 84 patents if you just absolve me from infringing on 63 of yours". And this system generally works quite well.

However, given the plethora of patents in such industries, the difficulty is that you seldom know in advance exactly which patents you will be infringing on; there are just too many of them lying around. What has now happened is that some specialized firms – the infamous "patent sharks" – have started taking advantage of this. They acquire patents not with the intention of using them, but with the aim to extort money from the unknowing infringers.

When a patent shark finds out that a certain firm is using a technology which more or less falls under one of its patents, it waits patiently until that firm has fully committed itself to the technology (and has incorporated it in its products, marketed them, made additional investments, etc.). Then the shark surfaces …

It will demand large sums of money for the infringement. If the firm refuses, they will roar "court action!" and threaten to shut them down. And the nice thing – at least, for the shark – is that the patent doesn't even have to be a really good one. Even if it is only a half-decent patent, with little chance of holding up in court, they can often convince a judge to issue an injunction, forcing the firm to suspend business pending the court's decision. And this can be so potentially disastrous for the firm that it quickly coughs up the dough to make the shark go away.

For example, NTP, a pure patent-holding company, filed a suit against RIM, the producer of the best-selling BlackBerry. RIM was confident that the five patents NTP was throwing at them would not hold up in court, because all of them had already been preliminarily invalidated by the US Patent and Trademark Office, while two of them had already received a final rejection, but when it seemed that a particular US district court judge (the Honorable Judge James Spencer) was inclined to grant the injunction, which would have cost RIM billions in lost revenue and lost competitive advantage, they promptly – but undoubtedly grudgingly – decided to hand over $612.5 million to NTP.

Getting scared already? I guess you should. There just might be some shark circling underneath, in your blue ocean … holding some obscure patent which could cost you an arm and a leg, if not more.

Information overload – and how to deal with it (if you're the one loading)

Knowledge in the management of corporations remains a tricky thing, and that is because it is such a fundamental topic – and raison d'être – for organizations. We're just a bunch of people working together and therefore we need to exchange and retain knowledge. Thus, most decisions in organizations require information. And usually we have to actively look for that information. We approach colleagues who have dealt with similar issues, are knowledgeable about the context, the customer or the technology, and try to incorporate their experiences and insights.

Nowadays, in our "knowledge economy", many companies have realized the value of this internal expertise and set up databases, accessible through the firm's intranet, that we can access and search. But now the problem is – more often than not – there is just so much of it!

We're swamped with information! How many databases can you access? How many documents can you read?! How many colleagues' brains and wisdom can you electronically pick?!

And this is actually not only a problem for the people looking for information. In many organizations the providers of knowledge are rewarded when others use their stuff, in the form of increased respect in the company, heightened status, and sometimes even in terms of hard cash after their annual performance evaluations. How can you as a provider make yourself seen and heard in the information quagmire?

Professors Morten Hansen and Martine Haas – at the time at the Harvard Business School – examined this issue. They examined the electronic databases of one of the Big 4 accountancy firms and surveyed its 43 "practice groups" on their strategy of what documents to upload and when. And they came back with some pretty clear insights into what works and what doesn't.

You have to understand that these different practice groups face some simple but concrete choices: how selective are we going to be in terms of the documents we upload; are we going to upload pretty much everything we get our hands on, or are we only going to put up a mere fraction of what we have? What is the maximum number of files we would like to put on to the system? Do we cover a fairly wide range of sub-topics or are we going to be much more concentrated in terms of the subjects we cover?

The trade-offs are pretty clear; if you upload very few documents, people can only access very few documents. But if you put up many of them, potential users may be turned off, can't see the forest for the trees and turn their attention somewhere else in disgust (while swearing at you for the sheer overload and making rude hand gestures to their computer screen). But where does the balance lie?

Hansen and Haas found out that where the balance lies depends on what topic you are publishing on. If the practice group was providing information on a topic that was being covered by quite a few other groups (such as, "cost management", "capital and asset management", "financing and IPOs"), they were much better off being very selective in what they put on their site. Those who made few documents available quickly gained a reputation as the group which always delivered high-quality stuff without swamping you with irrelevant, low-quality distractions. More people, as a result, accessed their pages.

In contrast, groups publishing on topics which were much less widely covered (such as "Peoplesoft", "hospital service delivery", or "call centres") were better off providing a much wider range of documentation, that readers could really sink their teeth into. They developed the reputation that "for topic X you really need to go to practice group A", and flourished as a result.

Hence, the various suppliers of information within the company competed with each other for the attention of the employees looking for relevant knowledge. And, like in any market, they needed to adapt their strategy based on the specific product they were offering.

When knowledge hurts

So there can be such a thing as too much knowledge. And having knowledge can also harm.

Over the past decade or so, companies have been told till it was a nuisance that their knowledge is their ultimate (if not only) source of competitive advantage. They have been encouraged – by management gurus, academics, and management consultants alike – that they should invest in knowledge development, protect it, and make sure it gets identified, codified, and even put on the balance sheet.

The advice was to carefully identify best practices and make sure that you have systems that help these practices to be shared throughout the organization. This way, you will make optimal use of the great good and surely a healthy return will follow – or so the preachers said.

Many companies responded, as advised, by setting up internal systems that could be used to store and access all sorts of documents, as well as systems to aid the identification of experts in the organization and ways to contact them for advice.

But have these knowledge management systems turned out to be as good as was promised to us? Well … let's say that a few caveats have emerged.

Because what we sort of forgot in the torrent of knowledge euphoria is that this stuff can also come at a cost. The cost of actually finding it, for example, in the jungle of corporate databases, but also the cost that comes with the fact that reusing prior knowledge doesn't necessarily make you very original. And that's a problem, especially when you need to stand out from the crowd.

Martine Haas and Morten Hansen also examined the use of internal knowledge systems by teams of consultants who were trying to win sales bids. They measured to what extent these teams accessed electronic documents and how much they sought personal advice from other consultants in the firm. They figured that, surely, accessing more knowledge must be helpful, right?

But they proved themselves wrong; to their surprise they found that the more internal electronic databases that were consulted by these teams, the more likely they were to lose the bid! Likewise for seeking advice from colleagues. This effect was especially pronounced for very experienced teams. These guys were much better off relying on their own expertise than trying to tap into experiences by others, whether it was in the form of electronic stuff or external advice.

Haas and Hansen figured that the opportunity costs of accessing all this prior knowledge must be huge; big enough to offset any potential benefits. Searching through the plethora of documents and soliciting advice from colleagues actually stopped the teams from making substantial investments into putting together a truly original and suitable proposal.

Things were even worse when competing firms were simultaneously bidding for the same lead, and so being able to differentiate yourself from these rivals became crucial. In these cases, utilizing prior knowledge seemed to lead teams to develop cookie-cutter solutions when being original and innovative was what was really needed. As a result, they lost the bid.

The only times that a team benefited from accessing internal knowledge sources was when it concerned a very inexperienced team. In such instances, talking to a few internal experts improved their chances of putting together a winning proposal. However, the internal document databases were always useless at best. The more these rookies tried to tap into the mountain of electronic documents available to them, they worse their chances of coming up with the winning bid.

The advice I derive from this research? Shut down your expensive document databases; they tend to do more harm than good. They are a nuisance, impossible to navigate, and you can't really store anything meaningful in them anyway, since real knowledge is impossible to put on to a piece of paper. Yet, maintain your systems that help people identify and contact experts in your firm, because that can sometimes be helpful. But make sure to only give your rookies the password.

Exaggerating to make my point

OK, I will admit to slightly exaggerating to make my point … Of course it would be silly to suggest, for example, that all electronic storage of documents is futile. However, I am quite serious about this bit: true in-depth knowledge about a complex system such as an organization and its competitive advantage is usually impossible to put on to a piece of paper. It often has a large tacit component that can't be articulated, let alone trans-ferred via some printed document; you really need face-to-face communication.

Professors Szulanski from INSEAD and Winter from the Wharton School wrote about this issue: "When it comes to complex systems, we found that no single expert fully grasps, and no set of documents fully captures, the subtle ways in which individual components are interwoven with one another."

For example, I have seen quite a few companies set up some form of acquisition database; business units or departments that had gone through an acquisition would put their models and documents on to an internal company database that other units can access, to prevent them from having to reinvent the wheel.

However, I really think these things are useless (if not dangerous) if done in isolation; the documents and models make little sense without the explanation or (even better) involvement of the individuals who created the knowledge in the first place. They can even be dangerous because they may create a false sense of security, because every acquisition is unique, and you may be following steps that, if taken out of context, do more harm than good, and because it prevents you from really tailoring and thinking things through. In such cases – when it concerns the transfer of abstract, complex knowledge – unless you accompany a database with a system to organize for human interaction, you may actually be better off without it.

R&D – it's a steal

One last question about knowledge in organizations, and that is about these knowledge-generation units called R&D departments: can you have a useful R&D department that is perfectly useless? Perhaps I should explain the question … Most R&D departments are supposed to generate new technologies, products, processes, etc. But not all do. Some R&D departments seem to never come up with anything that makes it to market. Clearly a waste of money, these lab-rats, right?

Well, maybe not.

For a long time, economists and other folks studying organizations assumed that R&D departments are supposed to come up with stuff. And only if they come up with good stuff – which eventually makes it into a sellable product and reaps a profit – is an R&D department worth the investment. Clearly, if they never come up with anything at all, that's money down the drain – or at least, that's what everybody assumed.

Then, two professors of strategy (note, not economists!), Wesley Cohen and Daniel Levinthal, discovered an interesting insight. To put it in a nutshell: sometimes, firms with R&D departments that never come up with anything at all still seemed to benefit

from them. How can such a seemingly useless bunch of Gyro
Gearlooses still be worth their while?

The trick is that, in many industries (and in most industries
to some extent), whatever firms invent comes into the public
domain, much like radio signals or air pollution. Hence, other
firms can easily access and imitate it. Economists always assumed
that this process is costless; you just pick it up and do it too.
Therefore, unless you're in one of those rare industries in which
patents really work, it's actually kind of nice if your competitor
invents something new; you can do it too without having had to
spend all this R&D money!

However, this turned out to be an over-simplistic view of the
world. Imitating your competitor is not that easy. It turns out
that firms that never invest anything in R&D actually have quite
a lot of trouble nicking ideas from others. They just don't quite
understand them well enough. In contrast, firms that do have
an R&D department – even if the geeks never invent anything
themselves – appear to be much better at copying others. That's
the unexpected benefit of having your own R&D: it equips you
to steal from others. Because of your investments in R&D, you
are better able to really understand the technology and apply it
in your own products and processes.

Wes and Daniel examined this phenomenon at length and wrote
a series of articles about it in a bunch of heavyweight academic
journals, with telling titles such as "Innovation and learning:
The two faces of R&D", "Absorptive capacity: A new perspective
on learning and innovation" and, my favourite, "Fortune favors
the prepared firm". It shows that there are two benefits from
investing in R&D: the first one is to invent stuff; the second one
is to build up the capacity to understand, assimilate, and apply
the things that others come up with in your own products and
technologies.

7

Making far-reaching decisions (when you can't see a fricking thing ahead of you)

The Red Queen

"[T]hey were running hand in hand, and the Queen went so fast that it was all she could do to keep up with her: and still the Queen kept crying 'Faster! Faster!' but Alice felt she *could not* go faster, thought she had not breath left to say so.

The most curious part of the thing was, that the trees and the other things round them never changed their places at all: however fast they went, they never seemed to pass anything."

> Have you read Lewis Carroll's *Through the Looking Glass*? If so, you might remember the passage above when Alice meets the Red Queen. They are running and running, but appear to be stationary. Competition among organizations can have the same effect. It is a race (whether in the mist or not). In order to keep up with competition, firms have to change continuously, in terms of adopting new technologies, launching new products and services, adapting to new business models, etc. Sometimes it really can feel like a race, and be quite exhausting.

"Suddenly, just as Alice was getting quite exhausted, they stopped, and she found herself sitting on the ground, breathless and giddy.

Alice looked round her in great surprise. 'Why, I do believe we've been under this tree the whole time! Everything's just as it was!'

'Of course it is,' said the Queen, 'What would you have it?'

'Well, in *our* country,' said Alice, still panting a little, 'you'd generally get to somewhere else – if you ran very fast for a long time, as we've been doing.'

'A slow sort of country!' said the Queen. 'Now, *here*, you see, it takes all the running *you* can do, to keep in the same place. If you want to get somewhere else, you must run at least twice as fast as that!'"

> **“ companies exposed to ongoing competition and change improved considerably and became much stronger firms 🙰**

Although quite exhausting – if you don't like running – it does make organizations better. Professor Bill Barnett, from Stanford, studied Red Queen effects among companies at length. He found that those exposed to ongoing competition and change improved considerably and became much stronger firms.

This is due to a "Darwinian effect" and a "learning effect". First of all, in such a race, the weakest firms go bankrupt, leaving only the strongest competitors. However, it also stimulates firms to learn and adapt quickly. And if you're learning and adapting, and becoming a more agile competitor as a result of it, this prompts your competitors to do the same (or die). It's a bit like an arms race … but one that consumers, and society as a whole, benefit from.

Bill documented another, long-term effect though; sometimes everybody is running in the wrong direction. Or at least, someone took a bit of a wrong turn and everybody followed. It is related to this thing I described at length in Chapter 2: the success trap; firms have been running in a particular direction only to find out that the world has just changed and some other corner of the market has become more attractive. This triggers the entry of newcomers, while the original leaders struggle to catch up, simply because they have advanced so far into the other corner of the world.

This is nothing new; we've seen it in the disk-drive industry, but also among freight companies using sailing ships when steamboat technology was introduced, among retail banks adopting innovative products and technologies, petrol stations evolving into self-service stations, with car-washes and mini-markets, in the steel industry when mini-mills emerged, tires in the automotive industry changing from bias to radial technology, and so on. The Red Queen is everywhere, and there are few places where you can afford to stand still. And if you want to get into such a race, look for an industry where everybody is running in the same direction; they're bound to get stuck in a corner some time soon.

Binoculars in the mist

The world of business is changing continuously. But the thing that is very difficult to predict is what will change and when; there is just a heck of a lot of uncertainty. And that makes making strategy a bit of a challenge ... Because how can you make proper plans with a ten-year horizon when you haven't got a clue what will happen in your business next year? It is a bit of a tussle ...

Therefore, my good colleague at the London Business School, Professor Don Sull – master of the analogy – often shows his classroom a picture of a sailor looking through his binoculars, saying, "This is our traditional view of how we regard making strategy": someone who is able to look into the future, and make a detailed plan of how to proceed towards a chosen destination. However, the reality of strategy-making is quite different; it is more – according to Don – like you're driving a car in heavy fog, peering through the window, trying to navigate around unexpected things that suddenly appear in your way.

> ❝ In businesses, although you may know where you're headed, the route is fraught with uncertainties and unexpected events. ❞

I like and agree with his analogy. In pretty much all businesses, although you may know where you're headed, the route is fraught with uncertainties and unexpected events. Technological developments, market demand, competitor actions, entrants, changing consumer preferences, Icelandic volcanos erupting, the macro economy, etc.: nobody can discern with any certainty what lies ahead of us.

I'd like to extend Don's analogy of driving in heavy fog. Because we're likely not alone on this road. We have competitors. And what do most of us do when we're sharing the road with other users in heavy fog? We concentrate on the lights of the car ahead of us, because it gives us some guidance, and we can rely a bit on the faith of the fella in front of us.

But, although it may make us feel more secure, is that really such a good idea? It's only human I guess, but it sometimes also seduces us to drive faster than we otherwise would have done, just to keep up with the advancing lights. And, if the fog is heavy enough, it seduces us to drive closer to the guy than we may deem wise if we'd thought about it. Of course, a multiple collision in the mist is quite common; we're following the car in front of us, but that doesn't mean that we can brake in time if he goes off a cliff, smashes into a tree, or another car on the road.

> **Competition is a race, but it's also a race in the mist.**

That's often how it goes in business as well. Competition is a race, but it's also a race in the mist. Often, everybody ends up following the quickest competitor, bidding for 3G licenses, entering China, merging with IT companies, etc. But sometimes, everybody ends up with a big bump on the head.

However, of course, if you slow down, you might lose the race. So, what do you do, confronted with fast-moving competition? Well, do what you do when you're driving in the mist. First of all, keep a healthy distance between you and the car in front of you. If he crashes, you still want to have time to stop. Second, if that car is driving faster than you're comfortable with, slow down. He may get there faster than you, but he may also not get there at all. And sometimes that's just not worth the risk.

Finally, don't use binoculars. They will blind you. Rigidly executing a detailed long-term strategy won't allow you to see anything unexpected in your way. You won't be able to navigate around – let alone take advantage of – the opportunities and obstacles that suddenly appear on the road ahead.

"Today's fast-changing business environment"? The same as it ever was!

But let's not exaggerate things. Sure, in most businesses there is competition, and in most businesses there is ample change. But most (if not all) "business thinkers" seem to not tire of proclaiming that the world is changing ever faster – and I am just not sure I am buying it.

Because you must have read it somewhere too: "Today's business environment is characterized by increasingly high levels of uncertainty and change" – or something like that. Half the articles in popular management magazines seem to start with a sentence like that. And, I have to admit, it annoys me. Deeply.

"In today's fast changing business world ...", "many industries are increasingly characterized by rapid change", "high velocity environments", "increasing hypercompetition", and so forth and so forth, blah blah, blah blah.

I know, it is slightly pathetic that something like this annoys me, but it does. I guess it annoys me because people simply accept it as a given, as the truth. But is the current business environment really so much more turbulent than it was when the world computerized, or when the Berlin Wall came down, or when electricity was invented? Somehow, I doubt it. But still, people always say that "the world of business is becoming increasingly volatile" (without showing me any evidence).

Fortunately, my fellow strategy professor Gerry McNamara, from Michigan State University, and two of his colleagues were equally annoyed but (in contrast to myself) did something about it. They analyzed the financial performance of about 5,700 companies over a period of more then two decades, looking at measures such as performance stability, market stability, abnormal business returns, industry dynamism, munificence, etc. And they found the following: nothing. Absolutely zilch.

Analyzing 114,191 observations from a variety of industries, starting from the late 1970s, they found that some lines of business may be turbulent, but no more turbulent than before. Or, as they say, "Our results suggest that managers today face markets no more dynamic and opportunities to gain and sustain competitive advantage no more challenging than in the past."

So please stop telling me that "the world of business is increasingly changing fast". It ain't. It is the same as it ever was.

Is innovation over-rated?

Let me now grumble at some other business press favorite: innovation. And the accompanying proclamations such as "innovation in today's business is key". Innovation is grand; innovation is what we should all strive for; innovators are always the heroes of the story. They saw the opportunity when no-one else could see it; they persisted stubbornly when everyone said they were a fool; they suffered hardship but eventually defied the odds to make it big, and so on and so forth.

And, granted, innovation is great. But we hear very little about the (undoubtedly many) poor sods who thought they were seeing something, but it really was just their imagination, who persisted stubbornly and foolhardily with something that was never ever going to work, who continued to suffer hardship till they vanished.

Do innovating firms perform better? Evidence from academic research on the topic is certainly equivocal: it is very hard to find solid evidence that firms which innovate (e.g., obtain more patents) perform better.

It so happened that I had a database of about 1,300 firms active in the Chinese pharmaceutical industry, and all their innovations. Note, innovations did not all have to be real blockbusters but could just be new types of products or applications. These new types could concern truly new drugs but more often they concerned a new dosage of some existing drug, a new intake form (e.g., pills versus injections), a new application of the same drug (i.e., a different disease for which a particular existing drug might also work), etc. Thus, not all of them were very radical innovations, but they were all new enough for them to have required clinical trials before their launch.

Using these data, I first tested, through some fancy statistical methodology, whether such innovations contributed to the growth of the firms over the subsequent years. The answer was a clear "no"; in fact, innovators grew more slowly.

Then I thought, "Perhaps they are innovating *because* they're running out of growth", so I applied a different (and even fancier) statistical technique to correct for that. Still, the answer was a resounding "no": innovators subsequently really had more trouble growing and this was a direct consequence of their innovations.

So then I thought, "Perhaps I am looking at the wrong thing; and I should not be looking at growth but at firm survival." Therefore, I changed my (already fancy) statistical methodology to test the impact of innovations on firm survival. But no, innovators died (i.e., went bankrupt) more often than non-innovators.

Then I thought, "Ah, it must be because innovation is risky; innovators may be the big failures of the industry but they are probably also the biggest success stories (I should really have thought of this earlier ... better not tell anyone ...)." So I used an even fancier statistical methodology to model not only the average survival probability of the innovators (vis-à-vis the non-innovators) but also their "variance". But no ... innovators really did fail more often than non-innovators, and with very little "risk"! In layman's terms: they died pretty quickly and you could be pretty sure of it. No risk–return trade-off here: the message is, do not innovate and you'll get a higher return for less risk!

So then I gave up.

Might the answer simply be that innovation is really not such a smart thing to do for a firm? It seems, as an organization, your chances of success are quite a bit better, and have less risk, if you simply stick to your knitting, or at least not try come up with new stuff yourself (but just wait patiently to imitate it).

> ❝ innovation really is great and, as a society, we need it ❞

But if that is the case, perhaps we shouldn't tell anyone ... Because innovation really is great and, as a society, we need it. But if everyone finds out that you, as an individual firm, are better off without it, people might not do it anymore ... So let's keep this one under wraps, and between you and me, alright?

Customers? Ah, forget about them

Let me quickly make amends for the prior section. I like innovation! Honest. I am just not so sure everybody should do it, and that everybody should be aiming for radical change. Paradoxically, in a turbulent business where the turbulence isn't caused by innovation (like the Chinese pharmaceutical industry), but by all sorts of other things, perhaps some of us are better off focusing on what we already do well, and doing it even better, rather than coming up with (even more) new stuff all the time.

But that does not take away from the fact that some of the greatest and most interesting companies in the world were – and are – very innovative. And that innovation can be very exciting. And that innovation can make you very rich – *if* done well (but that is a big "if" ...).

The aforementioned findings also suggest that not many companies that try very hard to be innovative succeed at it. That is why I regularly research companies that are great innovators. I am trying to figure out what they do that makes them successful.

How do they organize for innovation? What do they do differently than firms that do get stale, and sometimes even end up in a success trap?

This path also took me to a small dance company, called the Akram Khan Dance Company. The Akram Khan Company focuses on creating contemporary dance. It is small but extremely innovative (and extremely successful ...). I interviewed a guy called Farooq Chaudhry, co-founder and producer. Farooq had several interesting things to say about creating an organization that excels in delivering continuing, successful innovation. One thing that stuck to my mind was, "In order to be truly innovative, you have to forget about your customer."

What?! I don't know much about marketing (and would prefer to keep it that way), but don't these people always go on and on about "customer focus", "client-driven innovation", "the customer always comes first", and so on?

So I said, "Farooq, do you perhaps mean that you should only have the customer in the back of your mind?"

"No, no, I mean, customers – just forget about them altogether". OK ... What (on earth) did Farooq Chaudhry mean? After all, this is one of the most innovative companies of its kind, since ... well, like ever.

According to him, if you want to be truly innovative, you have to purposely not try to give the customer what he wants. Because, as he argued, if you set out to develop what you think the customer will like, you end up satisfying existing needs and tastes; you follow the customer, rather than leading him. True innovation, according to him, is about changing the tastes of customers, and giving them something that they have never seen or even imagined before.

I found his view quite appealing, and logically sound. If you really want to do something new, you might have to be brave enough to not ask people what they want, but to give them what they want (although they don't know they want it yet).

Means and ends; profits and innovation

My journey to study habitually innovative organizations also showed me that it is actually not easy to *remain* innovative. Sometimes firms come up with something really new, which brings them great success. But once the firm becomes profitable, over time, it is as if it loses the urge to be really innovative and creative, and come up with truly new products and services. I guess it relates to the phenomenon of the success trap, as discussed in Chapter 2. One innovation is doable; repeated innovation is another cup of tea.

In search of repeated innovators, one of the things I always ask a company's executives is, "Why do you want to be innovative?" Invariably, the answer is that they realize they need to innovate in order to remain profitable in the long run.

And this is a good point. You may be profitable now, but if you wait to invest in innovation till you see your performance dropping – trying to innovate yourself out of the trouble looming – it may be too late. True innovation has a long lead time; starting to think about new stuff only once your old stuff is beginning to show signs of decay often means you have left it too late. Moreover, by then, you may be out of touch; once you have stopped innovating it is very difficult to get back into it.

Over the past year or so, I have been examining a rather different but consistently very innovative organization – as a matter of fact, one of the most innovative organizations of its kind in the world: the famous Sadler's Wells theater in London.

Sadler's Wells is a large theater (its main auditorium seats about 1,900 people) which is focused on modern dance. And it hosts and (co)produces some of the most innovative productions in the world. Moreover, it manages to consistently attract large audiences and is – which is quite rare for such a theater – financially self-sufficient, very healthy and sound.

When I was talking to its managing director (Chrissy Sharp) and chief executive (Alistair Spalding) about its many productions, how they are organized, the relations between the theater and the artists, and so on, at some point I also asked them my usual question: "Why do you want to be innovative?" They both stared at me in silent disbelief …

While I was pondering whether they were wondering if I was serious (or mad), thinking it was just an incredibly stupid question, or considering stopping the interview immediately, Chrissy finally stammered, "But … because we have to … it is what we do."

Then it dawned on me; they had never even considered the question before.

And, gradually, speaking to many more people in the organization, I figured out that there is a subtle yet fundamental difference between Sadler's Wells commitment to innovation and that of many of the businesses I've seen. Companies invariably see innovation as a means to an end; you have to innovate in order to remain profitable. Sadler's Wells theater views it the other way around; you have to make a healthy profit in order to be able to continue to innovate.

For them, profit is the means and innovation the end. Companies often struggle to remain truly innovative when they are making huge profits; the urge and feeling of necessity just inevitably slips away. Not for Sadler's Wells; they continue to innovate, and innovate a bit more the more profit they make. It is not the big, tried-and-tested projects that they have been running for years that excite them, but the new, risky, creative productions that no-one in the world has seen before that get their hearts racing. They respect their established projects but invariably use the profit they make through those to invent new stuff.

> It is good to make a profit, and even better to make a lot of profit.

And I wonder whether more companies should adopt this stance: where the organization's ultimate commitment is to innovation. It is good to make a profit, and even better to make a lot of profit. But innovation is what keeps you healthy in the long run, and what generally tends to excite your people, employees and customers alike.

It is OK to get lucky – even for a top manager

Let me tell you a story about innovation. A story of a company called Hornby. If you're British, you'll know it. You might even be feeling slightly nostalgic merely thinking about it. Hornby makes model trains, and has been doing so for a very, very long time.

Ten years ago the company was nearly bankrupt. In an attempt to save costs it decided to outsource production to China. However, much to its surprise, it discovered the Chinese not only produced goods much cheaper, they also delivered superb quality. Therefore, middle managers could not resist spending all the money they were saving through the outsourcing on adding additional quality in their product designs and, most of all, a lot of extra detail: a working light on every table in the restaurant carriage, windscreen wipers on the locomotive, a bit of dirt (painted) on the bottom of the carriages, etc. Their products became perfect scale models.

Then, as much to their surprise as to their joy, they noticed sales increasing substantially. When it persisted, they started talking to their vendors to figure out what on earth was happening. They discovered that it was no longer fathers buying model trains for their children, but fathers buying them for themselves (and, in the process, spending quite a bit more money on themselves than on their children ...). Inadvertently, Hornby had moved out of the toy market into the hobby market, producing for collectors rather than children.

And they thought, "That's not a bad idea! Let's focus on that!" Not long thereafter, Hornby was outperforming the FTSE dramatically, seeing its share price rise from 35p to £2·50 in just a few years.

But what can we learn from a story like Hornby's? Isn't their smart change and innovative strategy simply due to sheer luck? Well, partly, but that's perhaps the first lesson. I find that many successful companies with great innovative strategies (e.g., Southwest Airlines, Zara, CNN) experienced some significant element of serendipity at their inception. But we (and often they) post-rationalize things as if it was all planned from the get-go.

But why? There is no shame in getting lucky. A great manager (such as Hornby's Frank Martin) does not necessarily come up with the strategy, but is superb at recognizing the opportunity when it comes knocking on the company's door, while subsequently carefully adding all the other necessary strategic elements (marketing, investor relations, distribution, etc.) to take advantage of the opportunity. Just recognize the importance of luck – rather than deny it – and make sure you gratefully take advantage of it.

" THE GOOD NEWS IS, PROFITS ARE UP 74%, THE BAD NEWS IS, WE DON'T KNOW WHY... "

Getting lucky – fortune favors the prepared firm

OK, let me tell you one more story. Once upon a time there was a plumber, called Geoffrey Ward, who lived in London. One day a local government official told him he would have to vacate his workshop and office because it was located in an area reserved as a retail zone.

Geoffrey decided to place an old, slightly exotic-looking, artistically shaped radiator, which he had removed for a client because it was broken, in the window of his workshop, just to make it look like a shop. In the following days and weeks, people kept knocking on his door asking whether they could buy that funny-shaped radiator. Soon, Geoffrey realized that he could have made a lot of money had he been able to sell such a "designer radiator" and decided to change profession. This was how the company Bisque, which produces and distributes designer radiators, was founded.

Luck, you say? Of course, but, as said before, many people don't take advantage of luck even when it is staring them in the face; Geoffrey did.

Andy Grove, former CEO of Intel, called it "strategic recognition capacity". He could have said "know when you got lucky" (but I'm sure you agree that that wouldn't have sounded as fancy). Intel, who of course became one of the most successful companies ever by producing microprocessors, also got lucky. In the early 1980s, they were working on microprocessors when they did not have a clue what they would be able to use them for.

They even made a list of potential applications – which included anything ranging from handheld calculators to lamp-posts. Yep, lamp-posts. What was not on it was the computer. It was not until IBM kept knocking on their door that they said, "Alright then, you can put our product in this thing you call a PC."

Yet, was this all down to luck? Of course not; Andrew Grove and his partners recognized the opportunity when it came knocking on their door (in the shape of Big Blue's rather sizeable fist). But there's more to it.

"Fortune favors the prepared mind", Louis Pasteur famously said. He got lucky several times, making important yet serendipitous discoveries (such as a rabies vaccine). Yet, it was not mere chance that it was Pasteur who made these discoveries: he recognized opportunities that presented themselves to him, but also had the skill, knowledge, and ability to turn them into something useful. That required many years of careful practice and training.

Moreover, and importantly, he wasn't sitting in his kitchen waiting for lucky events to fall into his scientific lap. He was actively experimenting with lots of things. Most of them were bogus; others not.

And that is what Intel did: running many experiments in the margin. Most of them failed and wasted money. But in your company, one sunny day, one of your experiments just might result in your own "microprocessor" and, if so, believe me, you won't shed a tear about all the ones that failed.

Sometimes it is about knowing when not to decide

OK, one more story then … And then I promise to stop, really.

Some time ago I was interviewing Tony Cohen, CEO of Fremantle Media; they own television production companies all over the world. A program developed in one country (say, *Pop Idol* or *The Price is Right*) may also have potential in another country. I asked him, "How do you decide which program is right for which country?" He said, "I don't".

"Why would I know any better than anyone else?" he continued. "I don't make these decisions." But he does make sure a system is set up that enables the organization to arrive at a good set of decisions. For example, each year, he organizes what is called the Fremantle Market. It is a one-day event in London, for which Fremantle executives from all over the world fly in. They present to each other their new television programs, which they have just had commissioned or developed pilots for.

I visited the event this year. Country executives really try to do a good job convincing their counterparts to "buy" their new television program, because Tony has made sure that if the new production of a Fremantle program in the Netherlands gets shown on television in the UK, the Dutch subsidiary receives a good commission that goes straight into their P&L. Moreover, the UK company is eager to obtain Fremantle's best new programs developed in other countries because if it manages to sell them to television broadcasters in the UK, it also makes a good profit.

Hence, Tony (or anyone else at Fremantle's head office) does not decide which program to invest in and promote as their next international winner, but he sets up the organizational system in order for local people to make their own decisions. This will enable their next global hit to emerge, without knowing in advance which program that will be. Sometimes he expected it; sometimes it's a program he never thought would see the light of day.

But often that is not the role we expect CEOs to assume. We expect them to make decisions quickly and without hesitation or even breaking into a sweat.

This story has reminded me of Andy Grove, when he was CEO at Intel. When Intel, in the 1980s, was in doubt about whether to concentrate on DRAM memory chips or on microprocessors, people (employees, analysts, shareholders, etc.) were banging on his door, saying "Please Andy, make a decision; are we going for DRAM or for microprocessors? Tell me what to do." But Andy said, "I don't know yet. No, I am not going to make a decision; let's see how things play out." Or, as he once confessed to Stanford Professor Robert Burgelman: "You need to be able to be ambiguous in some circumstances. You dance around it a bit, until a wider and wider group in the company becomes clear about it."

And that's what he did. He let individual middle managers make up their minds about what they were going to concentrate on. He gave the manager of their production plant a formula, in which he had to input a bunch of data concerning the market, margins, production efficiency, etc. and said, "This formula will tell you what to produce (because I don't know)." And gradually more and more middle managers started working on microprocessors (instead of DRAMs), and more and more the plant manager's formula told him to produce microprocessors (and not DRAMs). When the whole company had chosen microprocessors, Andy said, "Now I am ready to make a decision: we're going to be a microprocessor company." And everybody said "duh", because that's what they had been doing already.

I'd say his "indecisiveness" served Andy rather well, as Intel became one of the most successful and profitable companies in the world for the ensuing two decades: not by him making a tough decision quickly and decisively, but by not making it at all, instead enabling the organization to do it for him – just like Tony Cohen lets his organization decide what television programs to promote.

Retaining your ability to make money? Causal ambiguity's the answer

All this turbulence and ambiguity in the world of business of course makes life difficult. Things would be much easier if everything was nicely predictable and transparent, right? Wrong. Actually, if everything was unambiguous in our world, I doubt you'd be able to make any money. Let me explain.

Whenever people hear that I am a professor at a business school, the reply I most often receive is, "Oh, so you teach people how to make money?" And I usually nod while I display a weak smile and simmer in silence.

Some time ago though, I was teaching in New York, at Columbia University's business school, and took a taxi from JFK airport. The driver, making small-talk, said, "What do you do?"

"I am a professor at a business school."

"So you teach people how to make money?"

"Yeah (sigh), I teach people how to make money."

But then, the guy continued, "So, what's the answer?" That was a minor credibility crisis, right there on the spot!

I don't remember what I said, but I remember thinking later what I *should* have said. I guess it is about "creating value" (and selling it for more than it cost you to create) but also about "retaining value" (namely, why wouldn't anyone else be able to come in and do exactly the same thing – thus driving the price down till you can only sell it for what it cost you in the first place)?

And, of all business plans and proposals I get to see, people usually think a lot about the first bit: "how to create value". They talk about their unique value proposition, and why customers will love it, buy it, scream for it, and so on.

But they often forget about the second bit; why would *they* be able to do it, or at least do it better or cheaper than anyone else? What do they have or own that enables them to retain the value-adding ability, which protects them from immediate imitation by competitors?

For a start-up, that's often tricky. You don't have anything yet, so what could you possibly have or do that others couldn't do too? The trick is that you don't have to have it now, but you do need it a year or two from now, when you're starting to have a real business.

Thus, the thing that makes you "difficult to imitate" does not necessarily have to be a patent, brand name, unique location, etc. It could also be found in other sources; something that you build up over time. Over the years, I have found that one of the most powerful sources of being difficult to imitate is a rather mundane thing ... The firm's competitive advantage is difficult to imitate because the firm itself doesn't quite know what it does to be so good at it ...

We call this "causal ambiguity". It may sound silly but is surprisingly common. Firms, for example, see that they have a much lower cost base than their competitors, or they see that their salesforce is much more effective than theirs, or they manage to have a much lower error rate in their production process, but they don't quite know why ...

Causal ambiguity makes it difficult to put your finger on what it is you do that makes you so much better than your competitors.

But, don't worry about it: it's nice! When you don't know what it is you do, it will be difficult for your rivals to copy it and do the same.

SALES TEAM

LANG FOY GILL COOK

"WE'RE NOT SURE, BUT WE THINK FOY JUST DISAPPEARED INTO THE BUREAUCRACY."

Previously published in *Harvard Business Review*, March 2007

Company cloning – how to change a winning formula

When you realise you have a competitive advantage of sorts (because your performance is superior), a firm may often seek to replicate its success in other parts of the globe. However, that is easier said than done, if you do not quite know what you do that gives you this advantage. And then things can go horribly wrong, because the advantage might not be easy to export.

For example, I am sure many of you can name some of the ludicrous examples of when companies expanded into a foreign market and failed to adapt to the local circumstances.* It can be because they didn't adapt their product, their way of doing business, or even their name. For example, United Airlines famously handed out white flowers on flights from Hong Kong, where white flowers represent death and bad luck. India's M.P. Been Products printed a swastika on all their products sold in India (a symbol of good luck in many Far Eastern countries); this did not go down well when they launched German Pilsner, while Japan's Kinki Nippon Tourist Company noticed it attracted some unwelcome customers when it first expanded abroad.

And it's a perennial problem. Coca-Cola, when entering the Chinese market in the 1920s with less than moderate success, translated the sound of its name into Chinese characters, only to find out later that it, fairly unappealingly, translated into "bite the wax tadpole". Even further back, the British East India Company just might have lost control over India in 1857 when it continued to supply bullets encased in pigs' fat to its Indian soldiers, the tops of which had to be bitten off before they could be fired. Since it was against the soldiers' religion to eat pork, it seemed to have greatly whetted their appetite for pacifism.

The message that always comes with these examples is: "Adapt to local circumstances, stupid!" Don't just implement what you've been doing somewhere else, but implement an altered form of it, adapted to the local context.

Well, in spite of these examples, I am not sure that an immediate full-blown adaptation is the right path to glory …

Organizations and their business models are incredibly complex systems, consisting of many tangible and intangible

---

* See, for instance, David A. Ricks (2006) *Blunders in International Business*, 4th edn, Blackwell.

elements. And often we don't quite know what is causing their success – and, what's more, often people from the company itself don't quite know what is making it a success. Take the phenomenally successful Southwest Airlines. Is their success due to their swift logistics, the standardization of their procedures, materials, and airplanes, their coherent corporate culture, leadership style, recruitment procedures, etc.? We don't quite know: probably a combination of all of the above (and more).

> **❝ often people from the company itself don't know what is making it a success ❞**

Take Starbucks. Is it so successful because of the quality of its coffee, the training of its personnel, the layout of its bars, the logistics of the coffee-making processes, the ambiance, etc.? Well … probably all the elements interact, and create the competitive advantage together.

The problem with such a complex system is that when you change two or three elements of it, you don't quite know what will happen. Because all the elements interact, you may be screwing the whole thing up in ways you hadn't anticipated and won't even be able to untangle and understand.

Therefore, Professors Gabriel Szulanski and Sid Winter – from INSEAD and the Wharton School – recommend: "replicate". That is, before even thinking about making local adaptations, copy exactly what you have. Only once you've got it working, adapt it, very slowly, one step at a time.

Consider again Starbucks. It was originally replicated by its founder, Howard Schultz, modelled perfectly on an Italian espresso bar. "But it doesn't look at all like an Italian espresso bar!" you might shout. Very true. But the first one in Seattle did. There was standing-room only, full-fat milk, opera music, wait staff with bow-ties, etc. Only when Howard got that to work did he slowly start to make some alterations, through trial and error, one step at a time. Had Howard tried to make all sorts of adaptations right from the outset, it may not have worked at all.

The point of "replication" is not that you do not adapt to local circumstances, it is that you do not adapt from the outset. Rather than trying to create local perfection from scratch, first be cautious and modest: replicate exactly, get it to work to an acceptable level, and only then think about very gradually introducing some alterations. And then, eventually, you can still end up with a coffee bar that looks dramatically different from the original one in Rome.

When to fire your M&A management consultant

Because organizations are so complex, paradoxically you have to be slow to adapt, for instance when expanding abroad. Because no one mold fits all, you have to carefully figure out what the unique circumstances are, and what you should adapt when, in order to make it work and keep it working. This also brings me back to the topic of acquisitions, because they too are complex and unique creatures.

Some time ago, I gave a presentation to a group of executives from a variety of companies on the topic of acquisitions. Much of the talk was about how vastly different acquisitions can be, in terms of the purpose they are intended to serve. I ended my talk urging the executives that, if they ever came across a consultant who told them, "This is how you should integrate acquisitions" (promoting one particular method), they should fire him. Because acquisitions can be so enormously different in purpose and nature that they require fundamentally different approaches to integration, and if someone recommends a "one mold fits all" method, it is best to show that person the door.

Little did I know that the speaker coming after me was a consultant, armed with an impressive array of PowerPoints with titles such as "this is how you should integrate acquisitions ..." She looked a bit apologetic. Her company were also the main sponsor of the event ...

Anyway, I sort of mean it. Because sometimes acquisitions are intended to lead to consolidation in an industry, and the reduction of over-capacity (think for instance of Daimler and Chrysler). Sometimes acquisitions enable a number of companies to join forces, and benefit from some shared operations while remaining relatively autonomous (think for instance of Johnston Press, buying scores of local newspapers). Other acquisitions are intended as some form of substitute R&D (e.g., Cisco buying scores of entrepreneurial companies in Silicon Valley). Some acquisitions enable a firm to gain access to a new product or geographical market (e.g., Heineken buying local breweries), while yet others have to do with blurring industry boundaries (e.g., the various industry conglomerates, such as Viacom). Thinking that you could just treat them all the same way seems a bit naïve.

Now, it is of course true that, in all cases, you should "have a good communication plan", "integrate carefully", "make sure to not over-pay", and so on. But this type of advice is also a bit of a motherhood; after all, the professional life of a consultant (or strategy professor) recommending companies to "integrate poorly", "make sure you over-pay" and "have an appalling communication plan" would likely be swiftly truncated.

So what can you recommend? Well, first make sure that you understand what type of acquisition you're engaged in or, put differently, exactly why you are considering buying the company. What is it that is supposed to create all this surplus value? Once you have figured that one out, you might be able to deduce what can or needs to be preserved in the company, what needs to be integrated and what can be left to its own devices. Dependent on the outcome of that exercise, you can start to devise a further acquisition plan including, yes, a good communication plan, a careful integration approach, and a proportionate acquisition premium. And perhaps even a consultant.

Not all trouble is really trouble

While we are still on the topic of acquisitions, let me tell you another true story. Some time ago I was talking to a CEO regarding an acquisition his company had just done. The topic of "integration trouble" came up, and he said, "I've figured out how to avoid all such trouble; I just always quickly and completely assimilate the whole thing." And indeed, after acquiring the company he immediately merged it with the rest of the firm, spreading out all the new people across different departments and offices.

Shortly after that, I was talking to an executive (in charge of M&A) at another company, regarding "integration trouble". He said, "I've figured out how to avoid all such trouble; you simply have to leave them alone, and not meddle in." And that was what he did with his acquisitions; he bought them, but subsequently left them completely autonomous in all aspects of the business.

But who is right, and who is wrong? Hey, I am feeling in a positive mood: I am sure they're both right. Well … and both wrong …

Both strategies, indeed, usually manage to avoid severe integration tensions. Yet, they also prevent value creation. In order to create extra value, beyond the original two companies' worth, some form of integration will have to take place; otherwise you're just owning the two companies like any shareholder owns stock (you just happen to have bought it at a very high price!). Similarly, completely assimilating both units will destroy any potential for value creation, since you're eliminating all differences between the companies; simply increasing the scale of an organization will seldom result in much extra value. The differences you have just eliminated or ignored are the very source of the potential value that you need – at least to make the deal worth its while (i.e., its premium).

When Novartis, for example, was created out of the merger of Ciba–Geigy and Sandoz, subsequent CEO Daniel Vasella explicitly set up an integration program to create a new organization, which in many respects was entirely different from anything either of the companies had before. This approach doubled the company's value in about a year. Similarly, Igor Landau, former chairman of the merged pharmaceutical firm Aventis, said, "The strategy was to create a new company and not be the sum of the two previous companies. We decided either we create something new or we would pay the price down the line."

Acquisitions can be useful, but often only if they are utilized to create something new that the companies could not have done by themselves. Thus, it is tempting to avoid (integration) trouble, by either quickly and entirely assimilating an acquired unit or leaving it completely autonomous. But sometimes you have to bite the bullet; integration troubles can also be the symptoms of a much more healthy process, of organizational revitalization and the creation of new value.

Change for change's sake

When performed right, acquisitions might even help you out of a success trap – or prevent you from falling into one in the first place. Because once you're in such a trap, it needs quite a bit of stirring and shaking up trouble to drag you out of it. A similar role – and perhaps even better – can be played by reorganizations. Many of us have gone through one at some point in our lives, and my guess is you did not like it; you might not have seen its point, and found its logic dubious.

Have you ever worked for a company that changed its structure, and you couldn't figure out why? I did. Ages ago I was working for a consulting company that was organized by "function": consultants were grouped into departments defined by "strategy", "operations", "HR", etc. But then the company decided that it should really be organized by "industry", that is, group its employees into a division for fast-moving consumer goods, a division for government, heavy industry, professional services, etc.

And when people asked "why?", the company's management would come up with convincing answers for why it was beneficial for consultants working on the same type of customer to be grouped together. And people shook their heads in reluctant understanding and grudgingly eyed up their new colleagues.

But I couldn't help but think, "I could come up with equally convincing reasons for why this company should (still) be organized by function." And that is usually the case for most organizations. For example, you could easily come up with an explanation for why a bank should create divisions organized by geography; after all, people located in the same country often need to co-ordinate and have a joint manager. Yet, you could also come up with an argument for why they should be organized by product type; after all, people working on the same product (wherever in the world) should co-ordinate and learn from each other. Similarly, you could come up with valid reasons for why the bank should be organized by customer type; after all, big customers often want one point of contact, regardless of the product they require, and where they are in the world.

And I used to think, unless you can come up with very convincing reasons for why being organized by "industry" is now really more beneficial than being organized by "function", there is no justification for dragging everyone through a hefty reorganization.

> 66 I believe that reorganization is exactly what you should do (every now and then), even if it is unclear why. 99

But I've changed my mind. I now believe that dragging everyone through a hefty reorganization is exactly what you should do (every now and then), even if it is unclear why.

Let me explain. There is value in the process of reorganizing. Usually people in an organization should co-ordinate with other employees in their country, just like they should also co-operate with others working on the same product (wherever in the world), and others in the same function, etc. Yet, you're going to have to make a choice about what criterion you will use to organize your departments. Once you've, for instance, chosen to group people by function, inevitably, over the years, employees will start to identify with others in their function; their networks in the firm will be dominated by those people (because that is the people they interact with most), and gradually they may become insular, and not have much understanding or appreciation of people in other functions and departments, even if they are working on the same product or serve the same geographical market.

The trick to resolve this – or even avoid it, if you manage to do it proactively – is to simply swap them around. Break up the old functional departments and put them all together in departments defined by product (or whatever). The employees won't like it, because they think these other folks are a bit weird (if not dumb and whining) and they will tell you they felt quite comfortable in their old functional departments – which is precisely the reason you should change them!

Once people become comfortable in their groups, stop communicating and co-ordinating with others outside their department, and fail to see others' perspectives, it is time to turn them around. And the good thing is, for the first few years after the reorganization, they will still have their old social networks, perspectives, and knowledge of their previous, functional departments, while working with the new product structure. As a result, you can actually get the best of both worlds. And once they start to lose that, just change them again.

Now change it again!

Most firms change only in response to altering external conditions. Hence, they change because their old structure does not work anymore. I am suggesting that there is another reason for change: the creation of informal networks and a general awareness of what lies beyond a person's own departmental boundaries. The complementarities between the firm's informal social networks and its formal structure enable it to solve a co-ordination problem that most firms experience: namely that you have to also communicate with people outside your own department, and it is often difficult to get people to do that.

Actually, over time, while studying more firms and their reorganizations, I began to realize that there are two more reasons for change: (1) breaking escalated power distributions before it is too late, and (2) increasing a firm's capacity for change.

Different people and departments have different levels of power in every organization. And there is nothing wrong with that; there is an optimal allocation of power. However, as we know from research, power tends to accrue to people who already have it. Thus, power can get out of hand, beyond what is optimal! What I have noticed several successful companies and CEOs do is to alter such power structures before it is too late. They reorganize their companies before the power distribution becomes too skewed.

Furthermore, what we also know from research (but I am sure you may have experienced it yourself) is that, over time, firms gradually become a bit rigid and inert. Organizations, like people, get set in their ways. Altering the firm every now and then, through a reorganization, will restore a firm's general adaptability and capacity to generate and deal with change, which is key to success and even survival in many businesses.

But of course, notwithstanding the above, I recognize that there is a balance to be struck; you can also do too much of it. It is just that now, the predominant attitude seems to be to not change unless you really have to. I am just putting the burden of proof the other way around: change unless you have really good reasons not to, because there is value in the process of reorganizing.

"A serial changer"

In the process of learning about organizations and the benefits of regular reorganizations, I interviewed a guy called Al West. And Al is quite a guy. Not only because he is the founder and CEO of SEI, an investment services firm headquartered in Oaks, Pennsylvania, which has consistently showed earnings growth of 40 percent per year, but because of the way he runs his company.

For example, I asked for the contact details of his secretary to put an appointment in the diary. He doesn't have a secretary. Actually, he doesn't even have an office. And when I went to his London office to speak to him, reported at reception, and asked for Al West, the lady behind the desk said, "Who? Al West you say? Let me see if we have anyone in this company by that name." Al didn't strike me as the stereotypical autocratic, macho CEO.

What Al did strike me as – and which is the reason why I wanted to talk to him – is a "serial changer"; or at least that is how one of his employees described him to me. He is altering his organization – in terms of its structure, incentive systems, decision-making procedures, etc. – all the time, never quite satisfied and never quite done. And somehow, I suspect that is part of the key to his company's success.

In 1990, Al broke his leg in a skiing accident. He lay in the hospital staring at the ceiling for about three months. When he came back to work, despite the company growing and performing well, the first thing he did was to completely reorganize the entire firm. His employees thought, "Why change a winning formula? He must have been quite bored and couldn't think of anything better to do. I am sure it will pass." But it didn't pass. Ever since, Al has been reorganizing his company regularly.

And he does it because he doesn't want to allow his organization to become settled and "comfortable". SEI has been growing steadily for decades now, with an impressive – and impressively stable – 40 percent per year. Yet, Al never does any acquisitions (he feels they would disrupt the smoothly running organization). Unlike many other successful companies, SEI doesn't get trapped in its own success and gradually grow rigid and inert; SEI continues to innovate and grow.

The reason why many very successful companies find themselves in trouble in the long run is that they become too insular, narrow, and set in their ways. This leads to problems when their environment changes. Yet, Al's regular changes to his organization prevent it from becoming set in its ways. Moreover, powerful people and groups within an organization usually, over time, become even more powerful (because they can get their hands on even more resources, budget, and people): too powerful for the good of the firm. Yet, in SEI people don't get a chance to create fiefdoms and accumulate influence beyond what's good for the company. Al doesn't give them the time to do it.

That's what my good friends and colleagues Phanish Puranam and Ranjay Gulati found when they examined periodic structural changes within Cisco. They found that Cisco's many reorganizations helped to solve some tricky co-ordination problems within the firm. In many organizations, over time, employees become focused on their own unit, group or department. It's their perspective that they view things from; that's where their social networks lie, and whose interests they pursue. By regularly reshuffling departments, however, Cisco's people are not only forced to develop new perspectives and co-operate with other people, but the contacts and perspective of their old group (now dispersed across the firm) are also still available, so the firm gets the best of both worlds. Professors Nickerson and Zenger found similar patterns while examining Hewlett-Packard's regular switches between centralization and decentralization.

Regular changes to an organization may be perceived by people working in the firm as a pain (in all sorts of body parts) if not completely unwarranted ("We're performing well, aren't we? Why would we change anything?") but it helps avoid more serious trouble in the long run.

All of this ties back to the very first chapter of this book, namely how firms – especially the very successful ones – really make strategy. It is not a rigid set of decisions; it is something that emerges from the organization. In uncertain, foggy environments – and show me an environment that isn't! – firms can't plan everything and expect it to work. But you can organize – and reorganize – your firm in such a way that you can rely on it working well, and coming up with the goodies in some way or another.

"Innovation networks" and the size of the pie

The inevitable unpredictability of our world necessitates firms to organize in such a way that they will behave in equally unpredictable ways: hence, using some of the characteristics described above. However, the characteristics of how to organize do not merely concern the firm's internal features, but also concern how it connects to the outside world, for example through innovation networks.

"Innovation networks" is becoming a bit of a corporate buzzword so I write this with some level of embarrassment, but it happens to be one that (to my slight disappointment) I actually believe in.

More and more companies I see and talk to seem to realize that it is difficult to be innovative on your own. For true innovation, almost by definition, you need a wide variety of capabilities, knowledge, and insights. It is difficult to find such diversity within one organization. If you, as a firm, are trying to come up with fundamentally new things, you would likely do well to look outside your organization's boundaries, to see whether anyone knows anything that might be useful to you.

This is what "innovation networks" are about; combining and tapping into other companies' knowledge resources to, collectively, come up with something that neither firm could have done by itself. IBM, for example, does this consistently and in a highly structured way, working with specific partners on specific projects. Some of these partners are from outside their industry but others could even concern straight competitors. For example, in their Cell Chip project, developing multimedia processors, they work with Sony, Toshiba, and Albany Nanotech. In their Foundry R&D project, designing manufacturing processes for cell phone chips, they work with Chartered, Infineon, Samsung, Freescale, and STMicroelectronics. And they have several other similar projects, with yet different groups of partnerships.

However, networks can also be of a more informal nature. For example, the successful Sadler's Wells theater in London that I described earlier, which focuses on the creation of ground-breaking modern dance, has no orchestra or ballet of its own. Instead, it tries to create innovative modern dance shows by putting artists in touch with each other who otherwise would not have worked together. It organizes dinners during which those artists meet; it gives them some studio time and budget to improvise and experiment, and assists them with advice and other facilities to get them to combine their skills and talents to create new forms of modern dance. What they ask in return is that the artists premiere their performance in Sadler's Wells.

The most striking example of informal innovation networks I have seen, however, is that of Hornby, the iconic British producer of model trains and Scalextric slot car racing tracks. They have some more or less formal alliances with software producers and digital electronics companies, which for instance led them to develop virtual-reality train systems and digital slot car racing tracks (allowing multiple cars in lanes, which can overtake each other; clearly the most common schoolboy dream since the emergence of Samantha Fox!). Yet, they also have some informal networks, which stimulated their innovativeness. For example, one of their latest innovations is a real steam train (which retails at a whopping £350), and I mean real steam. The little whistler doesn't run on electricity but on actual steam. The interesting thing is how they came up with it. But, actually, they didn't ... One of their customers did. They maintain close networks – online, by organizing collector clubs, tournaments, etc. – with their collectors. Through these networks, they learned about a hobbyist who had invented a real model steam train. They went to visit him and adopted his rudimentary technology.

But the most striking example of their informal innovation networks I saw when I visited Frank Martin, Hornby's CEO, at the company in Margate some time ago. In his office lay a piece of slot car racing track. "Look," he said, "A very innovative and sophisticated new surface, which is not only much more realistic but also much less slippery for the toy cars. Our Spanish competitor sent it to us." I said, "What?! Why would your competitor do that? Are you sure it is not a fluke? Are you paying them for it?" And he replied, "No, whenever they invent something new, they send it to us. And we also send them stuff." I offered to try to explain to him the meaning of the word "competition" but to no avail ...

Hornby has no contracts or any other formal arrangements in place for these exchanges, and I have to say, I understand why it makes sense. They just figure, "We could shield our innovations from our competitors, but we're all much better off if we share them." The size of the pie (the total size of the market) will increase as a result of it, and they all benefit, much more than they would if they all kept their innovations to themselves.

It is a peculiar type of innovation network, if your customers and even competitors become part of it and share their innovations with you, purely on the basis of trust and reciprocity, but it is a formula that works for Hornby. It has managed to quintuple (I had to look up this word) its stock price over the past few years, partly as a result of such innovations. Innovation is important to many companies in many businesses, too important to (merely) leave to your own devices.

Spinning clients – the McKinsey effect

If you're really apt (or perhaps I should say shrewd), you can even create your own network – and even a network of customers, using your own employees. It is the McKinsey way.

Some time ago I had lunch with three McKinsey consultants and they started talking about how different all the people in their organization were. I was watching them during this conversation and couldn't help but notice that they even looked alike … They spoke alike, dressed alike and, clearly, thought alike. What seem like huge differences within a group may be miniscule (or even non-existent) if you're an outsider looking in.

It reminded me of a scene in Monty Python's *Life of Brian*, in which Brian looks out of his window and sees a huge crowd gathered in front of his house waiting for him to speak. And he shouts, "You are all different!" After which they dutifully reply in chorus, "Yes, we are all different." Brian: "You are all individuals!" Chorus: "Yes! We are all individuals!"

(I particularly like the guy who subsequently says "I'm not" …)

Anyway, McKinsey, like many highly successful individuals and organizations – my great colleague Professor Dominic Houlder tends to call them the most successful religious order since the Jesuits – attracts scorn and admiration in equal measure. But I believe they do many things right. One of them is that although the average person only stays with McKinsey for three years, when you join, you pretty much become a McKinsey person for life. If you "leave", you become an alumnus.

And that is a great feeling to foster if you, as an organization, lose most of your employees to your customers, because those people become great advocates for The Firm. McKinsey, for instance, proudly showcases them as alumni (although they have been able to keep remarkably quiet the fact that Enron's Jeff Skilling was among their most promising offspring …). Importantly, what do these alumni do, as soon as they start to work in the real world? Yep, they hire McKinsey consultants …

And these type of beneficial effects do not only accrue to McKinsey; other organizations can reap them too. Professors Deepak Somaya, Ian Williamson, and Natalia Lorinkova, for example, examined the movement of patent attorneys between 123 US law firms and 109 Fortune 500 companies from a variety of industries. They found that if one of those Fortune 500 firms recruited a patent attorney from a law firm, subsequently that law firm would start to get significantly more business from that company. And I am sure it works that way for many other types of companies too.

In addition, Deepak, Ian, and Natalia also found the reverse: if the law firm hired a person from one of the Fortune 500 firms, the business it received from that company tended to go up too! Moreover, if the law firm poached an attorney from one of its competitors, it saw business go up from the companies that were on the books of that attorney's previous employer. Apparently, customers often follow a job-hopping attorney to his new law firm.

Therefore, like McKinsey, perhaps you shouldn't be too frightened of people moving. You want to hire people from your competitors and your clients, but you may also want your clients to hire yours. Rather than vilifying them for leaving and cutting all strings, keep them on the books as alumni, and actively cultivate relationships with them, in the form of clubs, Christmas cards, and summer-evening barbecues if necessary! The only thing you don't want is for your people to move to your competitors ... They too may take business with them.

Hence, people will move: if they do, just make sure it is to a (potential) client – that's the McKinsey way. And, of course, make sure to keep quiet if they mess it up over there (like alumnus Skilling did at Enron) – that's also the McKinsey way.

8

A rock or a soft place?

The hidden cost of equity

What's all the fuss about being a public company anyway? I recently asked the CEO of a FTSE 250 company, "What's the advantage of being listed?" She shrugged and said, "I don't know; it can give you access to some capital I guess but, apart from that ...".

Of course it sounds rather sexy and exciting. Many CEOs don't just want to be a CEO; they want to be the CEO of a public company. But what are really the advantages of having your company listed on the stock exchange? Naturally, selling equity is a source of money, but of course there are other sources of capital which could suffice for your investment plans. But, alright, I'll give you that; it's one potential source of money.

Yet, I would say this source comes at a cost. Investment bankers will be able to spell out to you – in much too much detail – what the advantages and disadvantages are of the various sources of capital, including equity. However, I think they're forgetting one.

I recently spoke to Bill Allan, CEO of THUS (the former Scottish Telecom). Some years back, all of a sudden they were elevated into the FTSE 100. He admitted that, at once, he found himself having to spend the majority of his time dealing with fund managers, analysts, investors, the business press, etc. Of course this was a relatively unusual and extreme situation; the telecom bubble launched THUS into the FTSE 100 when they weren't quite ready for it. However, all the CEOs of public companies that I have talked to, in private, will admit that they spend about 30 percent of their time dealing with "the stock market" (i.e., fund managers, analysts, institutional investors, and the wider public). They wouldn't have to do this if they weren't listed.

Think about it: that's quite a cost. If you have a good company and you decide to float it (start to sell equity on the stock market), all of a sudden, you lose 30 percent of your top management capacity!

Are you sure that's worth it? That's 30 percent which you could have spent on cultivating your organization, motivating employees, thinking through opportunities for future growth, integrating acquisitions, etc.

Moreover, many CEOs end up not particularly enjoying the 30 percent ... It is a lot of hassle, pressure and a bit of a pain, having to tell (and defend) your "story" over and over again, to people who really don't have much in-depth knowledge about the company and its business, often haven't received any training in developing or even understanding strategy, and occasionally may not have much talent for or affinity with it anyway!

❝ being listed isn't so sexy and exciting after all ❞

How do you quantify this cost of being listed? I don't know; it is difficult to put a number on such a thing (which is probably why we don't pay much attention to it in the first place!). But I will assure you that many CEOs will privately tell you – albeit while whispering behind their hand – that being listed isn't so sexy and exciting after all. And, if they still had a choice, they would do without it.

"Shareholder value orientation" – now, where did that come from?

If you become listed, nowadays, the words "shareholder value" will likely become the most prevalent words in your vocabulary.

Because that is the prime, ultimate thing that you are supposed to be aiming for. But where did this thing – "shareholder value orientation" – come from in the first place? Well, there is an easy answer to that: it came from the US. And, partly from the UK.

For the (blissfully) ignorant among us, what is it? It is the view that the purpose of a public corporation is to maximize the value of the company for shareholders. Traditionally, we find this orientation in Anglo-American societies. The view that the public corporation is more a social institution which has to consider the interests of various stakeholders, including shareholders but also employees, customers, the local community, etc. is the traditional soft stuff found in other parts of Europe and Asia (although, over the past decade or two "shareholder value orientation" has been spreading like a forest fire – pardon the analogy – gaining geographic terrain even in previously unlikely homes such as Germany and France).

Whenever I ask a group of executives or MBA students in my classroom, "To whom is the primary responsibility of a company?", nine out of ten people will wholeheartedly shout "shareholders!", with usually a minority contingent on the back-burner – with a suspected long-term marketing indoctrination – arguing that "the company should adopt a customer focus" and always place customers first (because that's the best thing to do in order to gain shareholder value ...).

But why is that? Why do we immediately assume that the primary beneficiaries of organizations should be shareholders? I even find that quite a few people become annoyed, if not angry, by even the question being raised – like it is some God-given truth, which can't be opened up for debate and is embarrassing to think (let alone talk) about.

Don't get me wrong, I am not saying that companies shouldn't do it but surely it is not a "law of nature" that a company is ultimately (only) responsible to its shareholders. It's a choice. And as with many choices in business, that means that it is something worth thinking about every now and then: whether it is really the choice you want to make.

My former colleague (the great) Sumantra Ghoshal – who unfortunately died some years ago – would even argue (if inebriated) that shareholders are not owners at all, at least not of the company. He would argue something like the following (and a posthumous pardon to Sumantra if I remember his argument slightly incorrectly; he would often not be the only inebriated party taking part in the conversation …): He'd say, if you own a dog, and the dog jumps into your neighbor's house and wrecks the place, you are responsible for all the damage. However, if you own shares in an oil company and one of its oil-tankers shipwrecks and causes a billion dollars' worth of damage to the environment, you're only responsible for the extent of the monetary value of your shares; that's the maximum you can lose.

Although Sumantra of course realized the legal reality of the situation, his argument was that a shareholder's ownership rights are just as limited as his responsibilities. As a shareholder, you're an investor, which gives you the right to, for instance, dividends, but it doesn't make you the "owner" of the company in our traditional sense of the word.

Moreover, he would continue to argue that as an employee you often give a lot more: your intellectual capital, loyalty, ideas, firm-specific skills, investments, etc. And companies would do well to solicit such "gifts". And if as an employee you give a lot more (than just money), and a lot more of yourself, perhaps you're also entitled to more, in terms of the company's loyalties and priorities.

Who should come first? Shareholders? Are you sure…?

Herb Kelleher – the founder and former CEO of American icon Southwest Airlines – used to say: "We place our employees first".

It's a fairly extreme thing to say, especially in corporate America, that you do not place your *shareholders* first. Of course, he would always be quite quick to continue: "Because if you have happy employees, you will get happy customers, and if you have lots

" if you have happy employees, you will get happy customers " of happy customers, shareholders will inevitably become quite happy too."

Now you could be inclined to say, "Ah, so it's all the same; at the end of the day all parties' interests are aligned." And in the long run that may be true, but in the short run such an "employee orientation" – the choice of who comes first – can lead to rather different decisions than a "shareholder value orientation".

At Southwest they put their money where their mouth is; they, for instance, provide perfect job security. Consider, for example, Southwest's response to 9/11, which triggered a global airline crisis, prompting many companies to execute the hatchet on their employee headcount. Southwest Airlines' current president and COO, Colleen Barrett, said: "Southwest has not had a layoff in its thirty-year history and is not contemplating one now" (after which employees collectively organized an internal giveback effort, called "Pledge your Luv", offering up to thirty-two hours of pay during the last quarter of 2001).

In contrast, US Airways paid $35 million in lump-sum retirement benefits to its former top three executives, while 12,000 employees were laid off and pilots agreed to $565 million in concession in their own retirement plans. Rakesh Gangwas, briefly chairman and CEO (who received $15 million of the $35 million) declared, a few days before resigning, that "the September 11 attacks had allowed the airline to restructure and downsize in ways that would have been impossible otherwise".

Of course, US Airways filed for bankruptcy in 2003, while Southwest recovered in less than a year.

Placing employees first may be sub-optimal in the short run but in the long run it's a different picture. You don't become a better organization by having "better shareholders" (whatever that may be). You can most definitely become a better organization by having better employees. Truly prioritizing the well-being of your employees just might pay off financially in the long run too.

Loyalty, trust, extraordinary effort, etc. are reciprocal things; we give them to those from whom we receive similar. And organizations and employees are no different.

Human nature: self-interested bastard or community-builder?

It goes to the very nature of organizations, and of individuals. It pertains to why we co-operate in firms, and what motivates us as human beings. And I am not sure that in the world of business we have quite figured it out: how to align the fundamental aspects of human nature with work and motivation.

Allow me to elaborate: whenever I ask executives how they should make an organization more entrepreneurial, more customer-focused or simply more profitable they virtually always come back with: "incentivize people". Reward people for their ideas, their efforts and initiatives, and they will deliver.

❝ We evolved as being part of a tribe ❞

But always, when I ask them, if you were on a fixed salary, would *you* still do your best to come up with new ideas, be entrepreneurial, and deliver the best value you can for your customers? And then the answer is, invariably, "Yes I would, because I don't do it for the money." Then people say they like being good at what they do, initiating new things, and delivering customers the best they possibly can.

But why do we always assume that other people (but not *us*) are motivated – and motivated solely – by money, and the only way to get them to do stuff is by financially incentivizing them? No, we do things out of intrinsic motivation, because we want to do the best we can and contribute to the success of our firm. Is everybody really so different from us?

If you hadn't noticed; that was a rhetorical question.

So why do we assume other people are only motivated by money? My guess is it goes back to why we organize our firms the way we do. How we, in our society, organize our companies is basically based on two sources: (1) the Roman army (i.e., a hierarchy with unity of command), and (2) economics.

Economics has had a huge influence on how we govern our firms. For example, the use of stock options to incentivize and reward top managers comes straight out of "agency theory", and the spread of this practice has been linked to the spread of "agency theorists" across business schools in the US after which, gradually, the phenomenon started to diffuse. And there are other examples.

Yet, economics – including agency theory – works on the assumption that people are rational and self-interested. They will work if they are rewarded for it, but if they don't receive a direct reward or nobody can really observe their efforts, they will shirk and be lazy. Under this logic, indeed, you have to incentivize people; otherwise they won't do a thing.

And I guess to some extent, we are indeed rational and self-interested, and hence motivated by money. However, there is another fundamental aspect to our nature, one which through millions of years of evolution has made us the way we are: we like being part of a community and enjoy contributing to the well-being of that group.

Because we evolved as being part of a tribe. And people who were purely self-interested, shirking, and lazy would be kicked out of the tribe and clubbed to death, if not consumed for dinner. So our gene base evolved into making us slightly self-interested but also community-lovers. We all like doing things not only for our direct individual reward but also because it contributes to the community that we are part of. This community used to be our tribe. Nowadays, it is often our organization.

And if you, as a manager (i.e., headman) manage to tap into that deep fundamental need among your employees, you can build a powerful firm indeed. People love to do stuff that strengthens their firm, fulfills them with pride, and makes us feel stronger as a whole. We don't need to be financially incentivized to do that; it's our human nature.

Downtown Calcutta firms

By now, there is no denying it anymore, and I'd better admit it: I have a love–hate relationship with organizations. On the one hand, they're fantastic, and they produce things that no individual could have produced by himself, such as airplanes, open-heart surgery, and skyscrapers. However, on the other hand, they can be incredibly stupid. British Gas, which sends 28 letters and three bailiffs for a £100 bill despite having received evidence on multiple occasions that the meter is your neighbor's (as you may gather, this is not a hypothetical example!), Firestone, which continues to invest in bias tires while the whole world (including their own employees) understands radial technology is the future, and Ahold, which continues to make acquisitions although even the most junior employee is starting to suspect things are getting out of hand.

Yet, the thing that I dislike most about large firms is that so many of my (very well-educated and intrinsically motivated) friends seriously dislike going to work on a Monday morning – because, despite the façade, corporate life is dull, repetitive and unexciting. I also think this is probably the clearest symptom that organizations are not making sufficient use of the potential of what is likely to be their most valuable resource: people.

But many large organizations would like to be more entrepreneurial and vibrant. And therefore, they send their employees on training programs and culture courses, in which they build sandcastles together, climb poles, play drums, or go line-dancing, to develop some positive team spirit, and provide them with entrepreneurial energy and creativity.

My favourite anecdote regarding this issue comes from my late and great colleague Sumantra Ghoshal, who used to tell executives that every year in August, during his children's summer holiday, he would take them to his native Calcutta for a month.

However, downtown Calcutta would be so humid and hot in August that he could not do anything else than lie on his bed and be sleepy all day. However, when he spent spring in Fontainebleau – where he lived for many years when he was on the faculty at INSEAD Business School – which is located right in the middle of a protected forest in France, he could not help becoming cheerful at seeing the flowers blossom: he would start to whistle a song, run through the forest, and leap up to grab a branch!

"The problem with large organizations," he'd say, "is that most of them create downtown Calcutta in summer within them. And then they send you on a training course to improve your creativity and entrepreneurial energy. But the problem is not me!" he'd shout; "Place me in the Fontainebleau forest in spring and you'll see that I have all the energy and creativity you'll ever need. I don't need a course; you need to change your organization."

Sumantra did not accept the negative view of human nature adopted in economics and, consequently, in the way we set up and govern the corporations in our society. He was convinced that humans want to be energetic, creative, and contribute to the well-being of their community (e.g. organization) but that the way most large companies are organized, following bad recommendations from bad (economics-based) theories, often prevents them from doing what they desire. It's not the individuals that need changing; it's our idea of the firm.

> **It's not the individuals that need changing; it's our idea of the firm.**

Pay inequality – good or bad for team performance?

Now, let me descend from this abstract cloud and discuss some real-life implications in the reality of management: paychecks. When you have a team of people working on a common task, who all fulfill a similar role in the team (like a football team, a string quartet, a team of engineers, etc.) should you pay them all pretty much the same, or would you be better off creating different levels of remuneration within the team?

This question can stir up a fair bit of debate, and I have heard it being argued one way and the other. "You should pay them all the same," some loudly proclaim, "because they're a team and you don't want to create envy and inequality within the group!" Others will bellow in agony: "But you need to incentivize people, stupid! Equal pay kills their motivation; you should pay more to people who (seem to) contribute more, to keep them happy while stimulating the others to better themselves!!"

And who knows whether it is one way or the other? The problem is, it is very difficult to research this properly, and find a conclusive and reliable answer. You'd need information on the exact remuneration of all people in a team, their individual performance, and their team performance, and have a whole bunch of identical teams to make meaningful comparisons. And that's easier said than done.

However, Professor Matt Bloom, from the University of Notre Dame, decided to give it a try. And to make sure that he had a clean research sample, with a whole bunch of similar teams doing the same task, for which he could collect all the relevant info, he chose major league baseball.

And, although a bit unconventional, that's perhaps not such a bad idea. I don't know much about baseball (and would prefer to keep it that way!) but I assume the rules are the same for everyone, the teams the same size, working on the same task, etc. Thus, Matt collected performance data on 1,644 players in 29 teams, assessing their individual performance through batting runs, fielding runs, earned run averages, pitching runs, player ratings and all this (for me) abacadabra. For team performance, he measured a combination of on-field performance and financial performance, using game wins and revenue and valuation data. This gave him measures for team performance and the individual performance of each member of the team.

Then he measured player compensation. The newspaper *USA Today* apparently publishes salary and performance incentives for all players, so he used that. Finally, he created an indicator of "pay dispersion", or how big are the differences in the levels of pay between the players on a team. Using this data, he computed whether clubs were better off equalizing pay, or differentiating their team's payment levels.

And, it turned out, it's the former: that is, baseball teams performed better if the salaries of the players were quite similar to each other. The larger the payment differences, the lower the individual players' performance, mostly so – perhaps not surprisingly – for the players receiving the lowest payment. But – perhaps more surprisingly – also the players who found themselves pretty high in the payment pecking order, receiving an above-average salary package, saw their individual performance being negatively affected by the pay dispersion within the team.

Finally, team performance: those teams with high pay differences among players had markedly poorer performance. It seems substantial differences in pay are more of a demotivator than an incentive, even for the majority of people who end up in the high payment bracket! And the team suffers as a result.

What really caused the 2008 banking crisis?

I would argue – as, I guess, so would Sumantra – that the 2008 banking crisis was not really a macro-economic problem, the result of inappropriate government regulation, failing watchdogs, or even top management greed. Instead, it is the epitome of the structural failure of management: a direct consequence of our erroneous ways of organizing large companies.

Actually, I would say that when you compare the 2008 banking crisis with the Enron debacle, with Ahold's demise, or even with the Union Carbide disaster in Bhopal in 1984, some surprisingly clear parallels emerge. From past chapters, you should recognize such elements as the success trap, over-exploitation, tunnel vision, intertwined links between CEOs, analysts and boards of directors, heavy bouts of imitation, bandwagons and hubris, all overshadowed by the vast wings of Icarus.

Because one central element in each of the disasters, including the banking crisis, stems from the division of labour and specialization within and across organizations. In the case of investment banks, financial engineers drew up increasingly complex financial instruments that, among others, incorporated assets based on the American housing market. Yet, the financial engineers didn't quite understand the situation in the housing market; the people in divisions and banks participating in the instruments didn't understand the financial constructions or the American housing market; and when it all added up to the level of departments, groups, divisions, and whole corporations, top managers certainly had no clue what they were exposed to and to what degree.

Similarly, in Enron, managers did not understand what its energy traders were up to; Ahold's executives had long lost track of the dealings of its various subsidiaries scattered all over the world; and Union Carbide's administrators had little knowledge of the workings of the chemical plant in faraway Bhopal. The complexity of the organization, both within and across participating corporations, which had grown as a consequence of over-exploitation, had outgrown any individual's comprehension and surpassed the capacity of any of the traditional control systems in place.

Another crucial role was played by the myopia of success. Initially, the approach used by the companies involved was limited and careful, while there were often countervailing voices that expressed doubts and hesitation when gradually less care was taken – there is certainly evidence of all of this in the cases of Enron, Ahold, and Union Carbide. However, when things started to work and bring in financial returns, as in the case of the banks, the usage of the instruments increased, sometimes dramatically, and they became bolder and more far-reaching. Iconoclasts and countervailing voices were dismissed or ceased to be raised at all. For example, in Ahold and Enron, the financial success of the firms' approaches suppressed any doubts about their business strategies.

This caused a third element to emerge: herds. It actually became improper not to follow the approach that brought so much success to many. In the case of investment banks, other banks and financial institutions that did not participate to the same extent as others received criticism for being "too conservative" and "old-fashioned". Investors, analysts, and other stakeholders joined in the criticism, and watchdogs and other regulatory institutions came under increasing pressure to get out of the way and not hamper innovation and progress.

> **" Enron was hailed as an example of the modern way of doing business "**

Similarly, Enron was hailed as an example of the modern way of doing business, while analysts (whose investment banks were greatly profiting from Enron's success) recommended "buy" till days before its fall. Similarly, Ahold's CEO Cees van der Hoeven continued to receive awards when the company had already started its freefall. All of these organizations' courses of action had been further spurned and turned into an irreversible trend by the various parties and stakeholders in its business environment.

Banks and their top managers were all but forced to imitate each others' over-exploited practices, till the whole herd went off the cliff, dragging the world economy with it in its fall.

The third sin

There was of course a fourth management factor that contributed heavily to the downfall. It's the factor that is related to what was on everyone's lips in the immediate aftermath of each of the aforementioned crises: greed. Somehow, all organizations and individuals involved seemed to have let short-term financial gain prevail over common sense and good stewardship. But in all these cases, avarice – or greed; the third Biblical sin – was not restricted to the few top managers who ended up in jail or covered in tar and feathers. Ahold's shareholders initially profited as much as its executives. Investors, politicians, and even customers shared equally in the early windfalls of Enron, likewise for the investment banks. Even the Church of England made big bucks investing in the financial practices they so heavily criticized in the days following the collapse of the system.

❝ The greed factor is built into the structure of the whole corporate system. ❞

The greed factor, however, does not stand alone; it is built into the structure of the whole corporate system. Traders are incentivized to concentrate on making money; top managers are supposed to cater to the financial needs of shareholders above anything else – opening themselves up to severe criticism if they don't – and customers are expected to choose the best deal in town without having to worry where and how the gains were created.

However, none of these parties actually see what lies behind the financial benefits, or where they come from. The traders just see the numbers, the investors only see their dividends and earnings per share, and the Church of England simply chose the best deal while the archbishops were unaware it amounted to short-selling. The high degree of specialization and division of labor both within and between the financial institutions may have revealed the result of the process, but showed no sign of how these profits were produced.

In combination, all these elements combine to create a system that escalates risky short-term strategies until it culminates in an irreversible course of action. Consequently, it becomes unseemly to do anything else. As in a pyramid investment scheme, everybody is interlocked and benefits until the whole structure collapses, sometimes with devastating consequences. The 2008 banking crisis is only unique in the sense that it did not concern one organization but a whole global sector of interlocked firms, due to the high degree of similarity between the various corporations and their business strategies, and the unprecedented extent of the financial linkages between them.

All these things point to one underlying cause: the structural failure of management. The management systems used to govern these organizations were unable to control the inevitable spiral towards destruction. Whether analyzing Enron, Ahold, Union Carbide in 1984, or banks in 2008, the striking commonality is the sheer inevitability of the disaster; each of them were accidents waiting to happen, given the state of the organization.

More rules and regulations, and more quantitative and financial controls, are unlikely to solve the problem and prevent similar events from happening in the future. All organizations and people involved in these cases, ranging from top managers to traders and customers, were governed and incentivized by means of quantitative and financial controls. However, today's businesses are too complex to be controlled by rules and financial systems alone.

Instead, organizations need to tap into the fundamental human inclination to belong to a community (such as an organization), including people's desire to do things for the benefit of that community rather than focus on their individual interests. These are still alien concepts in the City and on Wall Street today, where incentives are geared towards optimizing individual, short-term performance while company loyalty and a sense of community are all but destroyed by the financial incentives and culture in place. Yet, when such human desires to contribute to a community are artificially suppressed through narrow financial incentive schemes, weird things can happen – and the 2008 banking crisis certainly was one weird thing.

"Work–family initiatives"?! That's rather soft and fluffy, isn't it?

But how do you create a firm which is more of a community? Well, let me just pick one; what about "work–family initiatives"? Or does that sound rather soft and fluffy to you? Guess it does. It concerns stuff such as on-site childcare, flexible working arrangements, family stress initiatives, and other similar nonsense.

Which tough, self-respecting corporation would want to be associated with that? Or should they? I guess it might actually help companies to become more attractive employers, which should ultimately help performance. Hey, even the stock market might appreciate such a thing, right?

Some time ago, Professor Michelle Arthur, from the University of New Mexico, set out to examine stock-market reactions to the announcement of Fortune 500 firms adopting such work–family initiatives, which she collected from the *Wall Street Journal*. For example, one of them said, "IBM began a childcare referral service for its employees" or, "Procter & Gamble are broadening the scope of their family-friendly policies", etc. She found 231 of them and then, for each of them, tested the stock-market reaction to the announcement, through what in statistics is known as an "event study".

The results were clear. In the early 1980s, the stock market hardly reacted at all to such fluffy initiatives; if anything, the effect of the fluffy announcement on a firm's share price was slightly negative (−0.35 percent). However, that changed quite a bit in the 1990s. When in that period firms declared a work–family initiative, their stock price immediately jumped up, 0.48 percent on average. Now that may seem like peanuts to you, but if you're a $5 billion company, it means that even one such initiative would already immediately increase the value of your firm by $24 million. That's a lot of peanuts. And a lot of shareholder value.

I've long thought that, for example, an investment bank that was able to come up with a formula that enables people to have a real career without working 70 hours or even five days per week should be able to turn that into a momentous competitive advantage in their industry (and it actually doesn't seem that hard to do). But macho culture and self-delusion – and not much else – always seems to stand in the way of developing such a practice. What Michelle's study suggests is that such firms are simply stuck in the 1980s; nowadays even the stock market recognizes the sheer monetary value of work–family initiatives.

It's time to wake up, I'd say, and join the new millennium. Because if you don't, you're actually destroying shareholder value, and that's not a very macho and serious thing to do, now is it?

"I've decided to re-enter the workforce so I can spend less time with my family."

Corporate social responsibility – nice, but does it earn you any money?

The view of organizations as communities naturally spills over into the question of whether they should do good or even contribute to the larger community. The corollary question, "Should corporations actively invest in socially responsible stuff, or should they simply focus on making money?" continues to linger and re-emerge on the business agenda (especially, it seems, around the time that corporate socialites swarm to Davos).

People are then quick to shout, "But they are not two different things; behaving in a socially responsible way will, in the long run, also make you better off financially!" but, in spite of the latest tally of 225 academic studies trying to provide hard evidence of the existence of that relationship, proof of that statement is unfortunately actually pretty hard to find ...

And I say "unfortunately" because it would be nice if socially responsible companies were also financially rewarded for their honorable endeavors. But it is hard to provide solid evidence for that. For example, although we know from research that socially responsible companies are usually the better performers, the tricky thing is that, as we say, the causality often seems to run the other way around; once firms start to make a healthy profit, they start acting in socially responsible ways. If losses pile up, the responsible stuff is the first to go out of the door. Hence, socially responsible behavior does not make you a better performer; good financial performance leads firms to behave in more responsible ways. It seems it is a luxury behavior that we only indulge in if we feel we can afford it.

❝ good financial performance leads firms to behave in more responsible ways ❞

However, on the bright side, there is certainly no evidence that firms acting in socially responsible ways perform more poorly as a result! So, if it doesn't cost you anything, why not do it? Yep, you will have to spend a bit more money, not using suppliers who employ children to produce their stuff, recycling your toxic waste although you could legally have dumped it somewhere else, and invest in some services for your local community and the family of your employees, although you could have told them to bugger off and take care of themselves. However, these niceties may also appeal to your customers, to green investors, will make you more attractive as an employer, and so on. And apparently these costs and benefits seem to largely average out so at least there seems no reason not to be a good guy! However, it would still be nice if the socially responsible types were actually better off wouldn't it ...

Professors Paul Godfrey, Craig Merrill, and Jared Hansen, from Brigham Young University and the University of North Carolina, came up with a clever insight into why socially responsible types may be better off after all. They didn't just look at the social and financial performance of all sorts of companies, but decided to specifically focus on companies that got into trouble because of some negative event that had happened to them. This could be the initiation of a lawsuit against the firm (e.g., by a customer), the announcement of regulatory action (e.g. fines, penalties) by a government entity, and so on. Then they measured what happened to the share price of the company as result of the event. And the interesting thing was that how much you were punished by the stock market for the negative news depended very much on how socially responsible you were.

Firms that scored low on a social responsibility index saw their share price plummet if they had to announce a negative event. Firms with very good social track records did not see the same fall in share price. Paul, Craig, and Jared concluded that, apparently, your social responsibility reputation acts as some sort of an insurance; when something bad happens to you, investors conclude that you probably made a genuine mistake, and that you will definitely do better next time, and that there is nothing structurally wrong with you or to worry about. However, when you are much more of a social villain, the stock market washes its hands of you, drops its financial support, and makes your share price plummet.

Thus, good guys are better off after all. And the dollars you spent on being socially responsible are paid back and turn into profit, especially when you are in a rut.

Taking care: companies make love and money (if their shareholders let them)

Here are three things that you don't often see together: caring for the community and the environment; shareholder value orientation; and takeover protection mechanisms. Surely they can't have much to do with one another, can they?

Well, they have quite a bit to do with one another, or so it appears. Let me explain.

First of all, do we like it that firms can adopt takeover protection mechanisms (such as poison pill constructions)? "No, we don't!" shareholders proclaim in chorus, because the threat of a potential takeover is a great way to make sure that CEOs don't do anything that does not maximize value for shareholders. Remove that possibility and these bloody CEOs will do all sorts of silly things that are not in our best interest.

And I am afraid that is at least half-true ... And one of these silly things is attending to issues such as caring for the natural environment and the community. We – the wider public – may like it if corporations do that kind of stuff, but it is not clear that shareholders do; after all, caring for such soft stuff comes at the cost of the hard stuff: cash.

Aleksandra Kacperczyk from the University of Michigan examined this issue in a clever way. She examined 878 public firms in Delaware between 1991 and 2002. The interesting thing about Delaware is that in the mid-1990s, due to a series of court decisions, hostile takeovers suddenly became a lot more difficult. And what Aleksandra found is that, after that fact, Delaware companies started to pay a lot more attention to caring for the community and the natural environment. All of a sudden, it was safe for companies to do such things, without the threat of punishment hanging over them, by means of a hostile takeover by another company that thought it could make more money by getting rid of all that expensive soft stuff.

Did shareholders like it? Well, they didn't applaud the court decisions (to say the least) and the fact that now corporations could divert valuable cash to such silly things, but they had to accept it. But were they right: was it going to cost them money? Well, not exactly.

Aleksandra also measured what happened to the long-term shareholder value of the corporations that started to engage in the "fluffy" stuff. Shareholder value actually went up! The long-term market-to-book ratio of these firms started to rise as a result of these actions. The shareholders, in spite of their doubts, were better off.

A classic win–win situation appeared; being freed from the threat of hostile takeovers enabled firms in Delaware to do nice things for the community and the environment, which actually paid off in terms of hard cash in the long run. But there was one catch …

Aleksandra had a brainwave and decided to also look at what happened to the levels of executive compensation (in the form of salary, bonuses, and other annual remuneration perks) of the companies that found themselves shielded from the threat of hostile takeover: CEO remuneration went up! Apparently, now immune to takeover threats, top executives not only started attending more freely to the interest of the wider community but also to their own private interests. They let others share in the wealth, but they didn't forget themselves either.

Epilogue

The Emperor's new clothes

Of course, I don't know why you read my book. Actually, to be frank, I don't even know if you have read it at all, since it seems one of the first things many people read when they pick up a book is its conclusion. However, if you're not one of those, and you have read my book, I am quite confident that you will have liked it …

And I am confident of that because, well, first of all, if you didn't like it you probably wouldn't have made it to the end … (unless you're my mother) hey, it is called "selection bias", remember! However, there is a second reason, and that is because the people who have read my tales before have told me they liked them.

For example, when I first started gathering my thoughts I began writing them on a blog. Nothing fancy, just using some free software, without giving it much publicity. But, quite to my surprise – I had just started putting stuff online to collect my thoughts and force myself to write – I saw my readership snowball, people started commenting and e-mailing me, and the *Financial Times*, *Business Week*, the *Washington Post*, the *Seattle Times*, the *Harvard Business Review*, etc. started to quote from the blog.

And I wondered why … Till one of my readers wrote to me saying, "It is a very fresh, honest and atypical way to look at business/management issues that few people take the time to stop and analyze" and "it is a side of business seldom talked about". Then I realized that quite a few of my readers liked it because, for the first time, they had the experience of spotting that the Emperor had no clothes …

People read my stuff and thought, "There's a naked man in the street, wearing nothing but a crown!" And (for some strange reason) quite liked that thought.

I'm sure you know Hans Christian Andersen's famous fairy tale. It is the tale of two swindlers who pretended to be weavers: "they said they could weave the most magnificent fabrics imaginable. Not only were their colours and patterns uncommonly fine, but clothes made of this cloth had a wonderful way of becoming invisible to anyone who was unfit for his office, or who was unusually stupid."

They then convinced the Emperor to let them weave him his clothes for an upcoming procession. At the time the garments should be ready, the Emperor sent his most trusted advisor – an old minister – to go and inspect the clothes: "The honest old minister went to the room where the two swindlers sat working away at their empty looms. 'Heaven help me,' he thought as his eyes flew wide open, 'I can't see anything at all.' But he did not say so."

Several other officials came to "see" the clothes, but not one of them admitted to not being able to spot anything: "So off went the Emperor in procession under his splendid canopy. Everyone in the streets and the windows said, 'Oh, how fine are the Emperor's new clothes! Don't they fit him to perfection? And see his long train!' Nobody would admit that he couldn't see anything, for that would prove him either unfit for his position, or a fool. No costume the Emperor had worn before was ever such a complete success."

"'But he hasn't got anything on', a little child said."

The little child's observation was first dismissed with a smile, but it sent a whisper through the crowd, until the mood began to change, and finally the whole town cried at last: "But he hasn't got anything on!"

There is nothing wrong with being naked

And I guess that's really what this book is: it's a little boy shouting "He is naked!" Because the world of business isn't always what it pretends to be. Things aren't as rational, well-organized and well-oiled as we're told they are. And we sort of know that ... But we also don't want to be seen as "unfit for office, or unusually stupid".

I've seen people read my tales with a smile – honest. I saw them thinking, "He's right; the guy doesn't have any clothes on ..." And isn't it a neat feeling to acknowledge that? It sort of puts us in a club, don't you think? "The club of people who have spotted that he has no clothes on". Shall we tell others about it? Hmmmm, you know what, let them figure it out for themselves. When they do, I tell you, it will be quite a relief: "I am not unusually stupid after all; it is just how the world works!"

But let me add one thing: there is nothing wrong with being naked (it is just the crown that makes you look silly). The world of business runs as it does. It is sometimes silly, it doesn't always work, but let's at least admit that we are all naked, so that perhaps we can start changing some stuff when it gets cold.

Because some things do need changing. Over the past few years, we have seen that companies that at one point are the darlings of the stock market and the topic of many business books and management seminars often become the villains of the corporate world a few years later. For most people, it is difficult to separate the wheat from the chaff. How do you know the advice provided in a business book or seminar is fair and reasonable, or whether it comes from tomorrow's Enrons, Lehmans, and Worldcoms? Whose knowledge can you still trust? How do you know that today's advice and cases will not be soon heralded as the epitome of *mis*management?

I think that is why people seem to like my book too – although my publisher told me not to tell you this (she thought you'd be bored, and might stop reading, but, hey, it is the last bit of the book anyway!): it is based on rigorous research from management science, conducted at the top business schools from around the world. It is not some bullshitty book that tells you the author's personal view on how to make your organization scream, how to manage your way to the pot of gold at the end of the market rainbow, or lead your company (with vision!) into a glorious path of unabiding growth. Don't get me wrong, some of these "how-to" books based on personal observations are nice, interesting, original, and sometimes even useful, but personally I also like facts: what do we really know about how things work? And I guess I am not the only one.

But – admittedly – of course this book represents my personal view as well. Yes, it is based on solid research and verifiable facts, but I have chosen which facts to present to you and what research to report; because what goes on in the world of top business schools and management science sometimes also leaves you pretty naked … Not all research is good and useful, and worth presenting.

I made a selection of what I thought was intriguing and important, and that is what I put in this book. I offer it to you as my crown. Please wear it with pride (but for God's sake, put some clothes on!).

Literature

Chapter 1

Asch, S.E. (1956) Studies of independence and conformity: A minority of one against a unanimous majority. *Psychological Monographs*, 70(9): 1–70 (No. 416).

Banerjee, A. (1992) A simple model of herd behavior. *Quarterly Journal of Economics*, 107: 797–818.

Bikhchandani, S., Hirschleifer, D. and Welch, I. (1992) A theory of fads, fashion, custom, and cultural change as informational cascades. *Journal of Political Economy*, 100: 992–1026.

Burgelman, R.A. (1994) Fading memories: A process theory of strategic business exit in dynamic environments. *Administrative Science Quarterly*, 39(1): 24–56.

Denrell, J. (2003) Vicarious learning, undersampling of failure, and the myths of management. *Organization Science*, 14(3): 227–243.

Harvey, J. (1974) The Abilene paradox The management of agreement. *Organizational Dynamics*, 3(1): 63–80.

Kahneman, D. and Tversky, A. (1979) Prospect theory: An analysis of decision under risk. *Econometrica*, 47: 263–291.

Kaplan, S. (2008) Framing contests: Strategy making under uncertainty. *Organization Science*, 19(5): 729–752.

Mezias, J.M. and Starbuck, W.H. (2003) Studying the accuracy of managers' perceptions: A research odyssey. *British Journal of Management*, V(14) n1: 3–17.

Mizik, N. and Jacobson, R. (2004) Are physicians "easy marks"? Quantifying the effects of detailing and sampling on new prescriptions. *Management Science*, 50: 1704–1715.

Nolan, J.M., Schultz, P.W., Cialdini, R.B., Goldstein, N.J. and Griskevicius, V. (2008) Normative social influence is underdetected. *Personal and Social Psychology Bulletin*, 34: 913.

Scharfstein, D.S. and Stein, J.C. (1990) Herd behaviour and investment. *American Economic Review*, 80(3): 465–479.

Starbuck, W.H. and Mezias, J.M. (1996) Opening Pandora's box: Studying the accuracy of managers' perceptions. *Journal of Organizational Behavior*, V(17) n2: 99–117.

Westphal, J.D. and Bednar, M.K. (2005) Pluralistic ignorance in corporate boards and firms' strategic persistence in response to low firm performance. *Administrative Science Quarterly*, 50(2): 262–298.

Chapter 2

Amason, A.C. and Mooney, A.C. (2008) The Icarus paradox revisited: How strong performance sows the seeds of dysfunction in future strategic decision-making. *Strategic Organization*, 6(4): 407–434.

Brockner, J. (1992) The escalation of commitment to a failing course of action: Toward theoretical progress. *Academy of Management Review*, 17(1): 39–61.

Gibson, C. and Vermeulen, F. (2003) A healthy divide: Subgroups as a stimulus for team learning behavior. *Administrative Science Quarterly*, 48: 202–239.

Gilbert, C. (2005) Unbundling the structure of inertia: Resource versus routine rigidity. *Academy of Management Journal*, 48(5): 741–763.

Greve, H. (2003) A behavioral theory of R&D expenditures and innovations: Evidence from shipbuilding. *Academy of Management Journal*, 46(6): 685–702.

Hsu, G. (2006) Jacks of all trades and masters of none: Audiences' reactions to spanning genres in feature film production. *Administrative Science Quarterly*, 51: 420–450.

Janis, I.L. (1982) *Victims of Groupthink*. 2nd edition. Boston, MA: Houghton-Mifflin.

Kahneman, D. (2003) Maps of bounded rationality: Psychology for behavioral economics. *American Economic Review*, 93: 1449–1475.

Kahneman, D. and Tversky, A. (1979) Prospect theory: An analysis of decision under risk. *Econometrica*, 47: 263–291.

Miller, D. (1993) The architecture of simplicity. *Academy of Management Review*, 18(1): 116–138.

Sørensen, J.B. and Stuart, T.E. (2000) Aging, obsolescence, and organizational innovation. *Administrative Science Quarterly*, 45(1): 81–112.

Staw, B.M. (1981) The escalation of commitment to a course of action. *Academy of Management Review*, 6(4): 577–587.

Sull, D. (1999) Why good companies go bad. *Harvard Business Review*, 77(4): 42–50.

Chapter 3

Agrawal A., Jaffe J., and Mandelker, G. (1992) The post-merger performance of acquiring firms: A re-examination of an anomaly. *Journal of Finance*, 47: 1605–1621.

Alexander, R.D. (1979) *Darwinism and Human Affairs*. Seattle: University of Washington Press.

Barney, J.B. (1986) Organizational culture: Can it be a source of sustained competitive advantage? *Academy of Management Review*, 11: 656–665.

Bascom, W.R. (1948) Ponapean prestige economy. *Southwestern Journal of Anthropology*, 4: 211–221.

Boyd, R. and Richerson, P.J. (1985) *Culture and the Evolutionary Process*. Chicago: University of Chicago Press.

Carroll, G.R. and Harrison, J.R. (1994) On the historical efficiency of competition between organizational populations. *American Journal of Sociology*, 3: 720–749.

Datta, D.K., Pinches G.P. and Narayanan V.K. (1992) Factors influencing wealth creation from mergers and acquisitions: A meta-analysis. *Strategic Management Journal*, 13(1): 67–84.

Dierickx, I., and Cool, K. (1989) Asset stock accumulation and sustainability of competitive advantage. *Management Science*, 35: 1504–1514.

Durham, W.H. (1991) *Coevolution: Genes, Culture, and Human Diversity.* Stanford, CA: Stanford University Press.

Franks, J. and Harris, R. (1989) Shareholder wealth effects of corporate takeovers: The UK experience 1955–1985. *Journal of Financial Economics,* 23: 223–249.

Jensen, M.C. and Ruback, R. (1983) The market for corporate control: The scientific evidence. *Journal of Financial Economics,* 11: 5–50.

King, D.R, Dalton, D.R., Daily, C.M. and Covin, J.G. (2004) Meta-analyses of post-acquisition performance: Indications of unidentified moderators. *Strategic Management Journal,* 25: 187–200.

Sirower, M.L. (1997) *The Synergy Trap: How Companies Lose the Acquisition Game.* New York: Free Press.

Tsai, W. and Ghoshal, S. (1998) Social capital and value creation: The role of intrafirm networks. *The Academy of Management Journal,* 41(4): 464–476.

Vermeulen, F. and Barkema, H.G. (2002) Pace, rhythm, and scope: Process dependence in building a profitable multinational corporation. *Strategic Management Journal,* 23: 637–653.

Chapter 4

Billett, M. and Qian, Y. (2008) Are overconfident CEOs born or made? Evidence of self-attribution bias from frequent acquirers. *Management Science,* 54(6): 1037–1051.

Chatterjee, A. and Hambrick, D.C. (2007) It's all about me: Narcissistic chief executive officers and their effects on company strategy and performance. *Administrative Science Quarterly,* 52(3): 351–386.

Wade, J.B., Porac, J.F., Pollock, T.G. and Graffin, S.D. (2006) The burden of celebrity: The impact of CEO certification contests on CEO pay and performance. *Academy of Management Journal,* 49(4): 643–660.

Wagner, J.A. III and Gooding, R.Z. (1997) Equivocal information and attribution: An investigation of patterns of managerial sensemaking. *Strategic Management Journal,* 18, 275–286.

Wagner, W.G., Pfeffer, J. and O'Reilly, C.A. (1984) Organizational demography and turnover in top management groups. *Administrative Science Quarterly*, 29: 74–92.

Zaleznik, A. (1977) Managers and leaders: Are they different? *Harvard Business Review*, 55(3): 67–78.

Chapter 5

Abrahamson, E. and Park, C. (1994) Concealment of negative organizational outcomes: An agency theory perspective. *The Academy of Management Journal*, 37(5): 1302–1334.

Fleischer, A. (2009) Ambiguity and equity in rating systems: US brokerage firms, 1995–2000 *Administrative Science Quarterly*, 54(4): 555–574.

Hayward, M.L.A. and Boeker, W. (1998) Power and conflicts of interest in professional firms: Evidence from investment banking. *Administrative Science Quarterly*, 43(1): 1–22.

Lester, R.H., Hillman, A., Zardkoohi, A., and Cannella, A.A. (2008) Former government officials as outside directors: The role of human capital and social capital. *Academy of Management Journal*, 51: 999–1013.

McDonald, M., Khanna, P. and Westphal, J.D. (2008) Getting them to think outside the circle: Corporate governance, CEO advice networks, and firm performance. *Academy of Management Journal*, 51: 453–475.

O'Reilly, C.A., III, Main, B.G. and Crystal, G.S. (1988) CEO compensation as tournament and social comparison: A tale of two theories. *Administrative Science Quarterly*, 33(2): 257–274.

Porac, J.F., Wade, J.B. and Pollock, T.G. (1999) Industry categories and the politics of the comparable firm in CEO compensation. *Administrative Science Quarterly*, (1): 112–144.

Rao, H., Greve, H.R. and Davis, G.F. (2001) Fool's gold: Social proof in the initiation and abandonment of coverage by Wall Street analysts. *Administrative Science Quarterly*, 46(3): 502–526.

Sanders, W.G. and Hambrick, D.C. (2007) Swinging for the fences: The effects of CEO stock options on company risk-taking and performance. *Academy of Management Journal*, 50: 1055–1078.

Westphal, J.D. (1999) Collaboration in the boardroom: The consequences of social ties in the CEO/board relationship. *Academy of Management Journal*, 42: 7–24.

Westphal, J.D. and Clement, M.B. (2008) Sociopolitical dynamics in relations between top managers and security analysts: Favor rendering, reciprocity, and analyst stock recommendations. *Academy of Management Journal*, 51: 873–897.

Westphal, J.D. and Khanna, P. (2003) Keeping directors in line: Social distancing as a control mechanism in the corporate elite. *Administrative Science Quarterly*, 48: 361–399.

Westphal, J.D. and Zajac, E.J. (1995) Who shall govern? CEO/ board power, demographic similarity, and new director selection. *Administrative Science Quarterly*, 40: 60–83.

Zhang, X.M., Bartol, K.M., Smith, K.G., Pferrer, M. and Khanin, D. (2008) CEO on the edge: Earnings manipulation and stock-based incentive misalignment. *Academy of Management Journal*, 51(2): 241–258.

Zuckerman, E.W. (2000) Focusing the corporate product: Securities analysts and de-diversification. *Administrative Science Quarterly*, 45(3) 591–619.

Chapter 6

Benner, M. and Tushman, M. (2002) Process management and technological innovation: A longitudinal study of the photography and paint industries. *Administrative Science Quarterly*, 47(4): 676–706.

Benner, M. and Tushman, M. (2003) Exploitation, exploration, and process management: The productivity dilemma revisited. *Academy of Management Review*, 28(2): 238–256.

Cohen, W.M. and Levinthal, D.A. (1989) Innovation and learning: The two faces of R&D. *The Economic Journal*, 99(397): 569–596.

Cohen, W.M. and Levinthal, D.A. (1990) Absorptive capacity: A new perspective on learning and innovation. *Administrative Science Quarterly*, 35(1): 128–152.

Cohen, W.M. and Levinthal, D.A. (1994) Fortune favors the prepared firm. *Management Science*, 40(2): 227–251.

Denrell, J. (2003) Vicarious learning, undersampling of failure, and the myths of management. *Organization Science,* 14(3): 227–243.

Groysberg, B., Lee, L. and Nanda, A. (2008) Can they take it with them? The portability of star knowledge workers' performance: myth or reality. *Management Science* 54: 1213–1230.

Guthrie, J.P. and Datta, D.K. (2008) Dumb and dumber: The impact of downsizing on firm performance as moderated by industry conditions. *Organization Science,* 19: 108–123.

Haas, M., and Hansen, M.T. (2005) When using knowledge can hurt performance: An empirical test of competitive bidding in a management consulting company. *Strategic Management Journal,* 26: 1–24.

Hansen, M.T. and Haas, M. (2001) Competing for attention in knowledge markets: Electronic document dissemination in a management consulting company. *Administrative Science Quarterly,* 46: 1–28.

Henkel, J. and Reitzig, M. (2008) Patent sharks. *Harvard Business Review,* 8(June): 62–68.

King, A.S. (1974) Expectation effects in organizational change. *Administrative Science Quarterly,* 19(2): 221–230.

Sørenson, O. and Waguespack, D.M. (2006) Social structure and exchange: Self-confirming dynamics in Hollywood. *Administrative Science Quarterly* 51(4): 560–589.

Starbuck, W. (2006) *The Production of Knowledge: The Challenge of Social Science Research.* Oxford, UK: Oxford University Press.

Staw, B.M. and Epstein, L.D. (2000) What bandwagons bring: Effects of popular management techniques on corporate performance, reputation, and CEO pay. *Administrative Science Quarterly,* 45(3): 523–556.

Trevor, C.O. and Nyberg, A.J. (2008) Keeping your headcount when all about you are losing theirs: Downsizing, voluntary turnover rates, and the moderating role of HR practices. *Academy of Management Journal,* 51(2): 259–276.

Westphal, J.D. and Zajac, E.J. (1998) The symbolic management of stockholders: Corporate governance reforms and shareholder reactions. *Administrative Science Quarterly,* 43: 127–153.

Zbaracki, M.J. (1998) The rhetoric and reality of total quality management. *Administrative Science Quarterly*, 43(3): 602–636.

Chapter 7

Barnett, W.P. and Hansen, M.T. (1996) The Red Queen in organizational evolution. *Strategic Management Journal*, 17: 139–157.

Barnett, W.P. and Pontikes, E.G. (2004) The Red Queen: History-dependent competition among organizations. *Research in Organizational Behavior*, 26: 351–371.

Barnett, W.P. and Sorenson, O. (2002) The Red Queen in organizational creation and development. *Industrial and Corporate Change* 11: 289–325.

Bower, J.L. (2001) Not all M&As are alike – and that matters. *Harvard Business Review*, 79(3): 92–101.

Burgelman, R.A. (1991) Intraorganizational ecology of strategy making and organizational adaptation: Theory and field research. *Organization Science*, 2(3): 239–262.

Burgelman, R.A. (1994) Fading memories: A process theory of strategic business exit in dynamic environments. *Administrative Science Quarterly*, 39(1): 24–56.

Gulati, R. and Puranam, P. (2009) Renewal through reorganization: The value of inconsistencies between formal and informal organization. *Organization Science*, 20(2): 422–440.

McNamara, G., Vaaler, P. and Devers, C. (2003) Same as it ever was: The search for evidence of increasing hypercompetition. *Strategic Management Journal*, 24: 261–278.

Nickerson, J.A. and Zenger, T.R. (2002) Being efficiently fickle: A dynamic theory of organizational choice. *Organization Science*, 13(5): 547–566.

Somaya, D., Williamson, I.O. and Lorinkova, N. (2008) Gone but not lost: The different performance impacts of employee mobility between cooperators versus competitors. *Academy of Management Journal*, 51: 936–953.

Szulanski, G. and Winter, S. (2002) Getting it right the second time. *Harvard Business Review*, 80(1): 62–69.

Vermeulen, F. (2005) How acquisitions can revitalize companies. *Sloan Management Review*, 48: 45–51.

Vermeulen, F. and Barkema, H.G. (2001) Learning through acquisitions. *Academy of Management Journal*, 44: 457–476.

Vermeulen, F., Puranam, P. and Gulati, R. (2010) Change for change's sake. *Harvard Business Review*, 88(6): 70–76.

Winter, S.G. and Szulanski, G. (2001) Replication as strategy. *Organization Science*, 12(6): 730–743.

Chapter 8

Arthur, M.M. (2003) Share price reactions to work–family initiatives: An institutional perspective. *Academy of Management Journal*, 45(4): 497–505.

Bloom, M. (1999) The performance effects of pay dispersion on individuals and organizations. *Academy of Management Journal*, 42(1): 25–40.

Dawkins, R. (1976) *The Selfish Gene*. New York: Oxford University Press.

Ghoshal, S. (2005) Bad management theories are destroying good management practices. *Academy of Management Learning and Education*, 4(1): 75–91.

Godfrey, P.C., Merrill, C.B. and Hansen, J.M. (2009) The relationship between corporate social responsibility and shareholder value: An empirical test of the risk management hypothesis. *Strategic Management Journal*, 30(4): 425–445.

Hayward, M.L.A. and Hambrick, D.C. (1997) Explaining the premiums paid for large aquisitions: Evidence of CEO hubris, *Administrative Science Quarterly*, 42(1): 103–27.

Kacperczyk, A. (2009) With greater power comes greater responsibility? Takeover protection and corporate attention to stakeholders. *Strategic Management Journal*, 30: 261–285.

Index